True Riches

To order additional copies, please contact us.
BookSurge, LLC
www.booksurge.com
1-866-308-6235
orders@booksurge.com

True Riches

A Practical Guide To Building Wealth

Ray Traylor, CPA

2006

True Riches

TABLE OF CONTENTS

Preface and Acknowledgments   xi
Chapter One: Spiritual Intimacy with God   I
Chapter Two: God's Value System   5
Chapter Three: The Maturing Process   I3
Chapter Four: Biblical Principles of Prosperity   2I
• Wealth Comes From God   2I
• Faith and Obedience   25
• Meditation and Application   27
• Unity in the Cause of Christ   29
• Blessings Come Through Giving   3I
• Impart God's Blessing on Your Children   33
• The Sovereignty of God   34
Chapter Five: The Four Ingredients of Success   37
Chapter Six: Building Wealth Made Practical   4I
• Debt   4I
• Inheritance   47
• Self-Employment   5I
• Leverage: Apply What You Have   53
• Employ Manpower   54
• Utilize Capital   59
• Harnessing Technology   6I
• Capital Investments   65
Chapter Seven: Twelve Steps to Wealth   69
Chapter Eight: The Gift of Giving   8I
Epilogue: A Personal Invitation   83

This book is dedicated to my Lord and Savior, Jesus Christ, who died for me and all mankind so that we might inherit eternal life. May He use it for the furtherance of His kingdom.

PREFACE AND ACKNOWLEDGMENTS

This book's purpose is to provide practical advice for Christians who want to focus their attention on raising financial resources for the furtherance of the gospel of Jesus Christ. The guidelines and advice for building wealth which I will share in this book are not new. They come directly from the Scriptures and have been proven to be true over thousands of years in many different cultures. I have attempted to summarize those key principles which have brought success to many people. Thus, this book is filled with Biblical passages and examples from across time and cultures which illustrate God's eternal truths. The personal examples mentioned in the book are based on real life experiences of real people, but some of the details have been changed to ensure the privacy of individuals. I pray that you will act on these ideas and that God will bless you in ways that you cannot imagine today.

A book is not merely a creation by the writer. In many ways, a book is the culmination of the efforts of many people who have contributed to the development of the author. My case is no different. I am thankful for many people who have helped me formulate my understanding of these principles. I want to offer my thanks to:

My parents, Raymond and Johnnie Traylor who have encouraged me in the ways of the Lord and demonstrated many of these principles in daily life; Herschel Martindale, my former pastor and mentor, who brought many of these ideas into focus for me; Dr. Mark Schmidt and Dr. Jim Stobaugh, who gave invaluable help in editing this book; to my wife and family, who daily have been an inspiration to me to follow Christ and put God's Word into action in my life and last but not least, to Jesus Christ—my Lord and Savior—who has given me new life.

CHAPTER ONE

Spiritual Intimacy with God

Have you ever wished that you knew God's thoughts on a specific subject? I certainly have. Many times in my life I have asked, "What is God trying to accomplish through these opportunities?" or "What is God trying to teach me through these circumstances?" The Bible teaches that God wants to give us that type of insight into the practical affairs of life. He wants us to know what He values and understand His ways. We see this truth in Psalms 103:7. David states that God "made known His ways to Moses, His acts to the sons of Israel." God and Moses were spiritually intimate! Their friendship was so personal that God chose to reveal His ways to Moses. In contrast, Moses' fellow Israelites did not experience that same level of spiritual intimacy with God. They merely saw the result of His actions. The Israelites benefited from the results of God's actions, whereas Moses was entrusted with God's plan. The Israelites saw God's actions, but Moses understood why God acted the way He did.

David is another example of a person who had an intimate understanding of God's ways. He spoke of knowing God in Psalm 25:4-5a, "Make me know Your ways, O Lord; teach me Your paths. Lead me in Your truth and teach me..." David longed for the same kind of spiritual intimacy with God that Moses had experienced. He boldly asked God for it.

Jesus demonstrated the same spiritual intimacy with His heavenly Father in His prayer in John 17:25-26,

O righteous Father, although the world has not known
You, yet I have known You; and these have known that
You sent Me; and I have made Your name known to
them, and will make it known, so that the love with
which You loved Me may be in them, and I in them.

It is clear that Jesus understood God's purpose for His life.
When facing death, He asked His Father if there were any other
way that the redemption of mankind could be accomplished.
Since the Father's response was "No," Jesus resigned Himself
to death and obediently vowed "...not my will, but Thine be
done" (Luke 22:42). Jesus longs for us to have this same kind
of spiritual intimacy with God that He had. We can see this
in His words that are recorded in John 14:21, "He who has my
commandments and keeps them is the one who loves Me; and
he who loves me will be loved by My Father, and I will love him
and will disclose Myself to him."

Now, as in ages past, God will reveal Himself to people
who genuinely seek Him. That simple truth is life changing.
God wants to have a personal relationship with each of us and
to reveal His heart's desires to us. However, to find God's will
and wisdom on any subject we must be willing to make Christ
our Lord and do His will. The Almighty God will only reveal
Himself to those who come to Him on His terms. In John 7:17,
Jesus said,

"If any one is willing to do His will, he will know of the
teaching, whether it is of God or whether I speak from Myself."

Before we begin exploring the subject of accumulating true
riches in life, we must stop and ask: Am I willing to do God's
will no matter what the cost? If not, then we will never know the

truth about true riches. Before we proceed, will you pause and tell God that you are willing to do His will no matter what it costs? Will you ask Him to make known His ways to you and will you seek to obey His wisdom?

When people do not submit to God's will, they will be alone as they make vital decisions which will affect themselves and their families. Without God's help, many mistakes will be made. Proverbs 14:12 states "There is a way which seems right to a man, but its end is the way of death." If we want to have divine wisdom for the decisions we will face in life, we must be willing to commit to the all-knowing God who loves us more than we can imagine. Only He can make our paths straight and give us true success.

Bob surrendered his will to God as a teenager. He dedicated his life to the Lord's service. As he was faithful to God's calling, he experienced the reality of God's presence. Even though he did not know where God was leading him, he was willing to follow. God honored this man's commitment, directed his steps and gave him success. During the last 50 years, God has blessed him, his business, his finances, his ministry, and his family. Today he is the leader of a national ministry and is a sought-after public speaker.

Now you face a similar decision. The Originator of the principles in this book, Almighty God, is waiting to interact with you. He wants to guide you as you apply His Word to the area of your finances. I believe that you, like Bob, will step bravely into the future and that Jesus will bless you beyond your wildest dreams.

CHAPTER TWO

God's Value System

In the 1970's Clint introduced me to the idea that God values people supremely. Clint taught me that as Christians our values systems should mirror God's. His father was a multimillionaire and Clint was the heir apparent to a sizable fortune. Not only was Clint born into wealth, he then became financially successful early in his adult life. As he matured, Clint realized that exclusively pursuing earthly wealth is unsatisfying and brings only fleeting happiness. He learned through experience that his values needed to be based on God's priorities. As Christians, we need to learn that same lesson. Our priorities need to shift from our natural, foolish desires to a reflect God's values. In Luke 12:13-34, we find many principles to guide us.

> Someone in the crowd said to Him, "Teacher, tell my brother to divide the family inheritance with me." But He said to him, "Man, who appointed Me a judge or arbitrator over you?" Then He said to them, "Beware, and be on your guard against every form of greed; for not even when one has an abundance does his life consist of his possessions." And He told them a parable, saying, "The land of a rich man was very productive. And he began reasoning to himself, saying, 'What shall I do, since I have no place to store my crops?' Then he said, 'This is what I will do: I will tear down

my barns and build larger ones, and there I will store all my grain and my goods. And I will say to my soul, 'Soul, you have many goods laid up for many years to come; take your ease, eat, drink and be merry.'" But God said to him, 'You fool! This very night your soul is required of you; and now who will own what you have prepared?' So is the man who stores up treasure for himself, and is not rich toward God." And He said to His disciples, "For this reason I say to you, do not worry about your life, as to what you will eat; nor for your body, as to what you will put on. For life is more than food, and the body more than clothing. Consider the ravens, for they neither sow nor reap; they have no storeroom nor barn, and yet God feeds them; how much more valuable you are than the birds! And which of you by worrying can add a single hour to his life's span? If then you cannot do even a very little thing, why do you worry about other matters? Consider the lilies, how they grow: they neither toil nor spin; but I tell you, not even Solomon in all his glory clothed himself like one of these. But if God so clothes the grass in the field, which is alive today and tomorrow is thrown into the furnace, how much more will He clothe you? You men of little faith! And do not seek what you will eat and what you will drink, and do not keep worrying. For all these things the nations of the world eagerly seek; but your Father knows that you need these things. But seek His kingdom, and these things will be added to you. Do not be afraid, little flock, for your Father has chosen gladly to give you the kingdom. Sell your possessions and give to charity; make yourselves money belts which do not wear out, an unfailing treasure in heaven, where no thief comes near nor moth destroys. For where your treasure is, there your heart will be also."

In Luke 12:13-34, a man asked Jesus to be an arbitrator between his brother and himself. Jesus wisely declined the man's request, but used it to bring the crowd's attention to God's real value system. In verse 15, Jesus explained that greed is a central problem in the heart of mankind. He wanted us to know that true living is not wrapped up in the type, quantity or quality of one's possessions. In contrast, Christ explained that His followers are to be consumed in seeking to further His kingdom on earth. As we seek first His kingdom, God is free to bless us in every way—including financially—so we can accomplish this task.

Jesus, the Master Storyteller, illustrated this principle in Luke 12:16-21. He told of a rich man whose life was totally consumed with the accumulation of wealth. It is clear from the story that this man's whole life and self-esteem consisted of his possessions. However, his life was cut short in the midst of his pursuit of wealth. After his death he discovered the shocking truth. He had accumulated riches which were not true riches! He stood in desperate poverty before the richest and most powerful King in the universe. How foolish he had been! He had sought the wrong kind of riches. In verse Luke 12:21, Jesus made it clear that this principle applies to everyone who "...lays up treasure for himself, and is not rich toward God."

In Luke 12:22-34, Jesus gave strong advice about accumulating wealth on earth. He made it clear that accumulating worldly wealth should not be our primary pursuit. If God feeds the ravens, and we are much more valuable than birds, will He not care for us? The implication is that God will certainly take care of our earthly needs. Jesus said that God supplies every need of the beautiful flowers of the field which are only alive for a short time. Certainly, He will adequately clothe His children. In light of these truths, we should not be consumed with the accumulation of worldly wealth, but we should devote ourselves to the matters which will further His Kingdom on earth. Too often we misdirect our energy, because we have misdirected our faith. We are trusting in money, not in God. In Luke 12:34, Jesus explained that what we accumulate reveals what we treasure in our hearts.

In a companion passage Jesus tells us to "seek first the kingdom of God and His righteousness and all these things will be added to you" (Matthew 6:33). From this passage we can see two things that God values highly: His kingdom and righteousness. The kingdom of God consists of people who have made Christ their King. In very simple terms, God values people more than anything else on the earth. Jesus Christ died to reconcile all people to God. This is stated in Romans 5:10,

"For if while we were enemies, we were reconciled to God through the death of His Son, much more, having been reconciled, we shall be saved by His life."

In God's value system, people are highly prized. Almighty God demonstrated this when He sent His Son to die for the sins of the human race. God also values godly character. We are commanded to seek first His kingdom and His righteousness. Our God is a holy God. He wants us to be holy people.

In view of God's values, we should devote our time, energy, and resources to reaching the most people for Christ's kingdom and developing godly character in their lives. If we value God's priorities, we are on our way to accumulating the true riches of life. These true riches are the people who make up His Kingdom and the character and holiness developed in their lives!

If true riches are people and godly character, how should the pursuit of worldly wealth fit into our lives? To answer this question, we again turn to the Scriptures. We will look at two chapters in the book of Luke that show God's perspective on eternal and temporal riches. In Luke 15 the Pharisees and the scribes were critical of Jesus because He allowed the tax collectors and non-religious Jews to come to Him for guidance. Jesus responded to their criticism with a series of parables. Each of these four parables is connected by this central theme: God longs for the reconciliation of every person on earth to Himself. God does not want anyone to spend eternity in hell. He would be thrilled if everyone would turn to Him for forgiveness and consecrate themselves to a holy life.

The first parable (Luke 15:4-9) tells the story of a shepherd who left his ninety-nine sheep in the fold while he went to find one which was lost. This passage recounts the shepherd's great joy when he found the lost sheep. Jesus compared the shepherd's joy to the rejoicing in heaven when one sinner repents and turns to God.

The second parable (Luke 15:8-10) is similar to the story of the lost sheep. In this story, a woman lost a valuable coin. She swept her entire house until she found it. When she finally found it, she was thrilled. In the same way, Jesus wanted us to know that God is overjoyed when a lost sinner turns to Him.

The third parable (Luke 15:10-32) is the well-known story of the prodigal son. This parable demonstrates the depth of one father's love for his wayward son who foolishly wasted his inheritance. The father was ecstatic when the son returned home to confess his foolishness and be reconciled to him. In the same way, God welcomes each person who turns to Him.

The fourth parable (Luke 16:1-13) is not often used in sermons or texts because it is more difficult to understand, but the passage can be understood in light of the preceding passages we just examined.

> Now He was also saying to the disciples, "There was a rich man who had a manager, and this manager was reported to him as squandering his possessions. And he called him and said to him, 'What is this I hear about you? Give an accounting of your management, for you can no longer be manager.' The manager said to himself, 'What shall I do, since my master is taking the management away from me? I am not strong enough to dig; I am ashamed to beg. I know what I shall do, so that when I am removed from the management people will welcome me into their homes.' And he summoned each one of his master's debtors, and he began saying to the first, 'How much do you owe my master?' And he said, 'A hundred measures of oil.' And he said to him, 'Take your bill, and sit down quickly and write fifty.' Then he said to another, 'And how much do you owe?' And he said, 'A hundred measures of wheat.' He said to him, 'Take your bill, and write eighty.' And his master praised the unrighteous manager because he had acted shrewdly; for the sons of this age are more shrewd in relation to their own kind than the sons of light. And I say to you, make friends for yourselves by means of the wealth of unrighteousness, so that when it fails, they will receive you into the eternal dwellings. He who is faithful in a very little thing is faithful also in much; and he who is unrighteous in a very little thing is unrighteous also in much. Therefore if you have not been faithful in the use of unrighteous wealth, who will entrust the true riches

to you? And if you have not been faithful in the use of that which is another's, who will give you that which is your own? No servant can serve two masters; for either he will hate the one and love the other, or else he will be devoted to one and despise the other. You cannot serve God and wealth"
(Luke 16:1-13).

When considered in the context of the preceding chapter, Luke 16:1-13 gives insight into God's perspective on finances. In Luke 16:1-2, Jesus told of a business manager who was caught squandering his master's possessions. The master reprimanded the manager and eventually chose to dismiss him from his duties. The errant manager realized that he was in serious financial trouble. In Luke 16:3-7, the manager took steps to ensure his future well-being at his master's expense. Before he was dismissed from his responsibilities, the manager called in several of his master's debtors and changed the amounts that they owed to the master. When the master found out what his manager had done he praised the manager for his craftiness. Luke 16:8 tells us that the master was impressed with his manager's foresight, even though it was to the master's disadvantage. This verse is easily misinterpreted. The master was not praising his manager for being unrighteous. He was praising the manager's resourcefulness, even though the manager's actions were wrong.

At this point, Jesus shows us His perspective on monetary riches. In Luke 16:10-13, He makes an important observation about His followers. He states that, generally speaking, unbelievers are more insightful than the righteous. Unbelievers are more open to opportunities around them. Jesus knew that unbelievers are prone to take advantage of their opportunities, but Christians often miss legitimate opportunities to advance God's purposes. In Luke 16:9, Jesus gave a straightforward directive to His disciples to use their riches to influence the most people for the Kingdom of God: "And I say to you, make friends for yourselves by means of the wealth of unrighteousness, so that when it fails, they will receive you into the eternal dwellings." From verses 10-13 of the same chapter, we can understand that Jesus considered money to be of little importance unless it was used for the glory of God. He considered it a tool to be used to advance the kingdom of God. In verses 10-13, He clearly indicated that the use of money is merely a proving ground to determine what lies in the heart of an individual. Jesus states that if we are not faithful with earthly riches, there is no reason for God to entrust us with the true riches of life. Here, as elsewhere in the Scripture, true riches are people!

From these passages we can see that God does not value material wealth for its own sake. Rather, He values people and the development of His character in their lives. We can see that material wealth should be used as a tool to reach the most people for Christ and promote godly character.

CHAPTER THREE

The Maturing Process

Billy was walking through the forest one autumn afternoon with his five year old son, Jason. Jason was full of questions as children always are at that age. Jason noted that some of the grass was taller than the small trees. His father explained that the tall grass would soon be dead and that the small trees would continue to grow next spring. Billy explained that for a short time the grass would be taller than the trees, but in the long run the trees would greatly overshadow them. Jason was amazed with the growth process. He asked, "Daddy, what will this small tree be like when it grows up?" Billy looked around and pointed out a giant 100 year old oak tree. He said, "Son this small tree can become just like that mighty oak tree." Jason's eyes became wide and he exclaimed, "God can really grow a tree!" In the same way God has a special purpose for Christians which takes years to develop. This chapter is about the maturing process which takes a lifetime, but produces strong and effective Christians.

God cannot use immature Christians to their full potential. In order to help us mature, He allows us to experience adversity. This process of spiritual maturing is called sanctification. As demonstrated in the following passages, God expects us to pursue righteousness and turn away from evil in order to become as useful as possible to Him.

"Everyone who names the name of the Lord is to abstain from wickedness" (2 Timothy 2:19c).

"Therefore, if anyone cleanses himself from these things, he will be a vessel for honor, sanctified, useful to the Master, prepared for every good work" (2 Timothy 2:21).

In order to rid us from the sins and misdirected priorities that hinder our service, God allows us to endure hardships. There are many Biblical examples of people who developed spiritual maturity through the trials they experienced. When we mature spiritually, we will be much more effective for God. This principle is illustrated repeatedly throughout the Scriptures. For example, the writer of Hebrews tells us that Moses

> ...refused to be called the son of Pharaoh's daughter, choosing rather to endure ill-treatment with the people of God than to enjoy the passing pleasures of sin, considering the reproach of Christ greater riches than the treasures of Egypt; for he was looking to the reward (Hebrews 11:24c-26).

At the time of his choice, Moses did not fully understand God's plans. He believed that God would use him to deliver the children of Israel, but he did not know the details. Chapters two through four of Exodus tells us how Moses relied on his own strength by murdering an Egyptian to defend one of his Hebrew brothers from oppression. Pharaoh heard of Moses' deed and sought to kill him, but Moses fled from the land of Egypt. Moses' self-confidence and courage melted away and he became a fugitive in the land of Midian. God intended to use Moses' circumstances to make him into an effective leader.

During the next 40 years, Moses experienced God's training program. God sought to produce a man who was no longer arrogant and self-dependent. God used the forty years that Moses spent on the back side of the desert to prepare him for a special task. No longer was he dependent on his own strength, but he humbled himself to do God's will. In Numbers 12:3,

"…Moses was very humble, more than any man who was on the face of the earth."

God had molded Moses' character until Moses could be trusted with God's greatest treasure: His people. From that point on, God used Moses as His representative on the earth. Moses had learned to submit his will to the Master and live according to God's plans and purposes.

The story of Joseph is another example of the way God develops a person's character before He puts him in a position of authority. In Genesis 37:1-11, God spoke to Joseph in a dream and revealed that Joseph would be a ruler among his people—even his father, mother, and all his brothers would serve him. The prophecy was accurate, but Joseph was not yet prepared to serve God in this way. He had been pampered by his father from his youth. Perhaps, he was arrogant about being his father's favorite son. At this time in his life, Joseph was not able to rule in righteousness and truth because of his undeveloped character.

Chapters 39-45 of Genesis tell how God allowed Joseph to be sold into slavery by his jealous brothers. Later, Joseph endured injustice and imprisonment. Through the dark times in his life, Joseph did not forget the revelations he had received from God. He patiently waited for God to fulfill His Word. Joseph learned obedience through the things he suffered. After Joseph's character was fully developed, God raised up the circumstances necessary to propel Joseph into a position of authority in the government. God forged Joseph into a man who was willing to do God's will no matter the cost. Joseph was then useful to his Master because he was prepared "…for good works" (Ephesians 2:10).

King David was another man whom God molded through

difficult circumstances. Before David could be king of Israel, God gave David many struggles to build his faith and his faithfulness. We discover from his comments in I Samuel 17:37 that David learned to rely on God during the earliest years of his life. When David was only a shepherd-boy, he fought to protect his father's sheep. In those experiences David learned to trust in God's strength. David states,

"The Lord who delivered me from the paw of the lion and the paw of the bear, he will deliver me from the hand of this Philistine..."

In the previous chapter of First Samuel, David was anointed King over Israel but was not given any instructions about when, where, or how he would take his rightful role as king. At that time, Israel already had a reigning king, so David had to trust God. Up to that point, every trial in David's life had been overcome successfully through God's help. David had been able to defeat Goliath, the champion of the Philistines with a sling and a single smooth stone. David held fast to his faith and believed God would continue to bless him. Time passed. It appeared that everything in David's life was leading to kingship. King Saul put David in charge of his armies. God gave him repeated victories over his enemies. The king promised his daughter in marriage to David. David ultimately became the king's son-in-law. Certainly everything was going David's way. He had no reason to be concerned that God's promise would not be realized.

But David's circumstances began to change. As he grew more powerful in the kingdom, King Saul became jealous and anxious. He made plans to eliminate David. Suddenly, instead of being a hero and a favorite son of the king, David was an enemy of the king and a hunted man. He no longer had a certain future, and he lived daily in fear of death. He beseeched God daily to spare his life. How the tables had turned! David was in utter despair, yet he continued to trust in God. He was so desperate that he cried out to God,

> My God, my God, have You forsaken me? Far from my deliverance are the words of my groaning. O my God, I cry by day, but You do not answer and by night, but I have no rest (Psalms 22:1-2).

In the midst of these trials, God was using David's circumstances to refine his character and develop his faith so that he would only trust in God. After David's training was complete, God gave him the promised kingdom. Then, David was entrusted with God's prize possession—His people.

This process of refinement is not limited to individuals. In the Old Testament, God was continually seeking to make the nation of Israel into a holy nation. He allowed many difficult circumstances to chasten His people when they turned away from Him. In the books of Joshua, Judges, Ruth, and the Kings God was continually sending adversity into the Israelites' lives, because they refused to follow His commandments. He hoped that they would turn away from their idols and turn to Him for deliverance. Some of the most obvious difficulties the Israelites faced included famine, pestilence, wars, and disease. Sometimes they responded to the discipline with repentance when they return to God, he blessed and delivered them. All too often, though, they failed the test and continued in their wicked ways. Of course, in those cases, their tribulations only intensified.

When the nation of Israel suffered in God's program of group discipline, the righteous members also suffered. Jeremiah provides a good example of a righteous man who suffered with a rebellious nation. From the story of Jeremiah, we can see that our personal well-being is not only dependent on our actions, but also on the actions of those with whom we are identified.

We have focused on how God uses discipline to refine us. However, there is another purpose for trials. Adversity may be simply a test of righteousness. Job was a blameless, upright, God-fearing man who turned away from evil. God was pleased with Job and blessed him materially. He was the richest man on the earth in his day. In Job 1:8, God was so pleased with Job's attitude that He boasted to Satan about Job's steadfast righteousness. God had confidence that no matter what hardships Job faced, Job would continue to trust his Maker. This observation began a cosmic struggle between good and evil with Job as the center of attention. Satan attacked Job with vengeance. God allowed Job to lose his family, his livestock, his riches, and his health. His wife became so discouraged that she told him to curse God and end his life. Yet, Job trusted God. Although he did not understand why God allowed the horrible circumstances, he knew that God loved him and that God was the Divine Controller of all circumstances. From the Biblical account, we know that these trials were tests of Job's character and faith. God used this process as a refining fire to develop and test Job's character. Throughout the trials, Job remained true to the Lord. Ultimately, God blessed Job with twice as many children, livestock, and riches.

In the New Testament, Hebrews 12:5-11 addresses this process of sanctification. This passage reveals two negative responses to God's discipline.

> And you have forgotten the exhortation which is addressed to you as sons, "My son, do not regard lightly the discipline of the Lord, nor faint when you are reproved by Him; for those whom the Lord loves He disciplines, and He scourges every son whom He receives." It is for discipline that you endure; God deals

with you as with sons; for what son is there whom his father does not discipline? But if you are without discipline, of which all have become partakers, then you are illegitimate children and not sons. Furthermore, we had earthly fathers to discipline us, and we respected them; shall we not much rather be subject to the Father of spirits and live? For they disciplined us for a short time as seemed best to them, but He disciplines us for our good, so that we may share in His holiness, all discipline for the moment seems not to be joyful, but sorrowful; yet to those who have been trained by it, afterwards it yields the peaceful fruit of righteousness (Hebrews 12:5-11).

God trains and disciplines His children to become godly people. He uses Biblical instructions and the circumstances of life to develop our character. Hebrews 12:5-6 encourages us to not regard God's discipline lightly or to faint when we are reproved by Him. These are the two normal responses to discipline.

First, when disciplined, we may choose to ignore it or to disregard God's urging. This response occurs when we believe that there will not be any negative consequences for our disobedience. However, the entire Bible gives us examples of the consequences for those who do not follow God's commands. When we disobey God, He allows sin to damage us and, even in some cases, to destroy us (Galatians 6:7-8).

The second negative reaction to godly discipline is to "faint" under it. To "faint" under discipline means that we decide that it is too difficult to obey the Lord. However, we are assured that God will not assign us a task that is too difficult. We are exhorted in Galatians 6:9 to "...not lose heart in doing good for in due time we will reap if we do not grow weary." In another passage, Moses tells us that God's commandments are not "...too difficult for you, nor is it out of reach" (Deuteronomy 30:11).

Hebrews explains that the process of sanctification is administered through the discipline of a loving, heavenly Father. The result of this training is a holy life. On a larger scale, the goal of this process is to produce a kingdom of holy people (I Peter 2:9).

Based on these observations, here are four essential principles that we should strive to incorporate into our daily lives:

1. We should seek to understand God's ways in order to please Him.
2. We should value people and godly character since these things are the true riches, rather than material wealth.
3. If we want God to be able to use us fully, we must cooperate with Him as He develops our character.
4. We must accept adversity as part of our maturing process.

CHAPTER FOUR

Biblical principles of prosperity

Wealth Comes From God

Helen was a hardworking wife and mother who wanted to have a Christ centered home. The only problem was that she was not at home very much. Like many struggling two income families, Helen was employed outside the home. It seemed that every month the family budget was always stretched to the limit, but yet she was convinced that God wanted her at home with her kids. After a couple of months, she told her concerns to her husband, Frank. Little did she know that God had been speaking to Frank about this same thing. Frank asked Helen if she knew of any job she could do at home. After some consideration, she mentioned that a couple of her friends had commented on the attractive drapes she had made for their home. She also remembered that her friends had offered to pay her to make some drapes for them, but Helen was too busy with work and family responsibilities. She thought perhaps this was the way God would allow her to be a helper to her husband while at home. After a couple of weeks of prayerful consideration, Frank and Helen agreed that Helen should try to develop the drapery business and see where God led. Within three months, Helen had enough orders to quit her regular job and work full-time at home. The business grew at home and become a source of income for the family while allowing Helen to minister at home where she felt God wanted her. As Helen and Frank followed God's direction for their lives, He blessed them abundantly.

> But you shall remember the Lord your God, for it is He who is giving you power to make wealth. That He may confirm His covenant which He swore to your fathers, as it is this day (Deuteronomy 8:18).

Often, people think that wealth comes from their own hard work and determination. The Bible gives us a different perspective. God is the one who gives us the strength, skills, and opportunities to gain wealth. Many people want to take the credit for their success and their wealth. They attribute their success to experience, wisdom, hard work, or inheritance. Sometimes they attribute their success to blind luck. However, Proverbs 10:22 tells us,

"It is the blessing of the Lord that makes rich, and He adds no sorrow to it."

God blesses His people with riches and wealth. There are also New Testament passages that bring this principle to light. James 1:17 points out that every perfect gift is from God.

> Every good thing given and every perfect gift is from above coming down from the Father of lights, with whom there is no variation or shifting shadow.

We should not take credit for what God has done. Another important passage on this subject is found in Psalms 112:1-6,

> Praise the Lord! How blessed in the man fears the Lord, who greatly delights in His commandments.

His descendants will be mighty on earth, the generation of the upright will be blessed, wealth and riches
are in his house and his righteousness endures forever.
Light arises in the darkness for the upright. He is gracious and compassionate and righteous. It is well with
the man who is gracious and lends, he will maintain
his cause in judgment, for he will never be shaken. The
righteous will be remembered forever.

God says that wealth and riches are in the house of this
man who delights in the commandments of God. Not only will
God bless him with riches and wealth, but with children who
will be blessed by God and successful on the earth. When we
take credit for our own wealth, we are being prideful. Prideful people cannot please God. James 4:6 says, "But He gives a
greater grace, therefore is said, 'God is opposed to the proud, but
gives grace to the humble.'"

In order to fully realize the value of riches and wealth we
must subordinate our desires to God's will. We must be willing
to let go of our wealth for His glory and His kingdom. In Mark
10, Jesus met a young man who was facing a decision about how
to use his wealth.

As He was setting out on a journey, a man ran up
to Him and knelt before Him, and asked, "Good
Teacher, what shall I do to inherit eternal life?" And
Jesus said to him, "Why do you call Me good? No one
is good except God alone. You know the commandments, 'Do not murder, do not commit adultery, do
not steal, do not bear false witness, do not defraud,
honor your father and mother.'" And he said to Him,
"Teacher, I have kept all these things from my youth

up." Looking at him, Jesus felt a love for him and said to him, "One thing you lack: go and sell all you possess and give to the poor, and you will have treasure in heaven; and come, follow Me." But at these words he was saddened, and he went away grieving, for he was one who owned much property (Mark 10:17-22).

Jesus wanted something more from this rich, young man. The young man was willing to outwardly obey God, but Jesus wanted a fundamental change in the man's heart and commitments. The young man's heart was still filled with his possessions. Instead of this man owning his wealth, his possessions owned him. The message in this passage is that when we allow the things of this world to become our focus, they soon possess us. In order for our possessions to be a blessing to us, we must surrender them to Christ and be willing to use them for His purposes. Like this rich young man we have the opportunity to use the wealth God has given us for His purposes.

We have already established that the true purpose of earthly riches is to advance the kingdom of God. The Apostle Paul gave us specific advice about how to apply God's value system to our choices: "Whether then, you eat or drink or whatever you do, do all to the glory of God" (I Corinthians 10:31).

Think of the many decisions we make daily, especially decisions concerning our finances. This passage says that we should do everything for the glory of God. Have you ever thought about how to use your money for the glory of God? The next verses tell us how to accomplish this goal.

Give no offense either to Jews or to Greeks or to the church of God; just as I also please all men in all things, not seeking my own profit but the profit of the many, so that they may be saved (I Corinthians 10:32-33).

God's goal is to bring as many people as possible to Himself. Paul personalized that goal and devoted all his resources to reaching it. We should use our assets to help accomplish that same goal. Paul stated, "I do all things for the sake of the gospel, so that I may become a fellow partaker of it" (I Corinthians 9:23). Paul tried to make every decision count for eternity. He used his energy, his money, and his resources in order to further the gospel of Christ.

Faith and Obedience

Robert was an enterprising young entrepreneur with a growing business. Like many new business owners, his business was undercapitalized at first. However, Robert believed that God had led him to open this business and in the early years of operation God blessed him with success. One day a missionary came to his church and spoke about the work that was being done overseas. Robert felt the Lord prompting him to participate in giving to that work, but he had just made enough money to fully capitalize his business. He was fearful that if he gave any amount to this mission work, it would put him back into the struggle he had just overcome. He decided instead to postpone his giving until he built up excess capital. He reasoned that if he gave now something might happen that would jeopardize his business. Over the next three months one disaster after another happened to Robert's business and he soon found himself undercapitalized again. As he tried to understand why his business had taken a turn for the worst, he sought advice from his pastor. During the discussion his pastor asked if there was anything that God had asked him to do that he refused to do. At that point Robert remembered the prompting of the Holy Spirit to give to the mission work overseas. The pastor gently pointed out that the blessings of God come through faith and obedience. At that point Robert could not give to the same degree he could have before. He examined his budget to see what he could do. He made arrangements to give according to his present abilities and committed to give in the future as God provided. Within six months Robert's business had recovered to the place that it had been when he first heard about the financial need of the mission work. God continued to bless him as he was faithful to do what God laid on his heart.

> Therefore the Lord longs to be gracious to you and therefore He waits on high to have compassion on you. For the Lord is a God of justice; how blessed are all those who long for Him (Isaiah 30:18).

God's desire is to bless His people, but He will punish and correct us if we willfully disobey His commands. If we believe and obey Him, He can pour out His blessings on us. God's blessings are the direct result of our sanctification. In Deuteronomy 5:29, God speaks about His desire to bless His people.

"Oh, that they had such a heart in them that they would fear Me and keep all My commandments always, that it may be well with them and with their sons forever!"

Once again we see that God's blessing comes to His people when they obey His word. According to the Scriptures, prosperity is linked directly to faith and obedience.

Meditation and Application

After graduating high school J.C. Penney went to work for a local dry goods merchant. In 1898, he began working in a small chain of stores called the Golden Rule stores. By 1902, the chain owners had offered him a one-third partnership in a new store Penny would open. Penney invested $2000 and moved to Wyoming to open the store there. After that he opened two more stores with the same partners. In 1907, his partners sold all three stores to Penney. Penney continued to expand his Golden Rule stores and by 1912 he had 35 stores in the Rocky Mountain states. In 1924, he incorporated the J. C. Penney Company and phased out the Golden Rule name. By 1916, he expanded the chain east of the Mississippi River. In the 1920's he expanded the stores nationwide. By 1929, he had 1400 stores. Later in life Penny explained his business philosophy. He felt that much of his success was tied to the fact that he meditated on Jesus Christ's words which are commonly called the Golden Rule, "In everything, therefore, treat people the same way you want them to treat you, for this is the Law and the Prophets" (Matthew 7:12). Penny meditated on this principle and sought to apply it to his business. He said, "I cannot remember a time when the Golden Rule was not my motto and precept, the torch that guided my footsteps." He also stated, "The Golden Rule finds no limit of application in business." It's not surprising that God blessed this man financially as he sought to apply God's Word in his business. In the following paragraphs we will examine the principles of success which are tied to meditating on and applying God's Word.

This book of the law shall not depart from your mouth, but you shall meditate on it day and night, so that you may be careful to do according to all that is written in it; for then you will make your way prosperous, and then you will have success (Joshua 1:8).

The word "success" only appears in the King James Bible in this verse. As humans, we are captivated by success. We would do well to understand God's perspective on this topic. God's formula for success is simply stated in Joshua 1:8. God wanted Joshua to know that in order to achieve success and prosperity he must follow God's guidelines. These same commands are applicable to us today. First, God's Word must be constantly on our lips. We must never stop discussing it with each other and exploring ways to put it into action. His Word must become the focus of our thoughts and meditation. This is a practical way to love God with our minds. As we think about His commands, God will show us ways to put them into action. Meditation is not merely for mental exercise.

God intends for His people to do all that is written in His commands. God rewards this careful obedience with prosperity and success. The first chapter of Psalms describes a person who continually meditates on God's Word as a "...tree firmly planted by streams of water..." This person will prosper even during difficult times because God's Word is his source of nourishment.

How blessed is the man who does not walk in the counsel of the wicked, nor stand in the path of sinners, nor sit in the seat of scoffers! But his delight is in the law of the LORD, and in His law he meditates day and night. He will be like a tree firmly planted by streams of water, which yields its fruit in its season and its leaf does not wither; and in whatever he does, he prospers (Psalm 1:1-3).

Unity in the Cause of Christ

Garrett was a business owner whom God blessed with an abundance of contracting work. Actually, he had so much work that he did not have adequate staffing to service the new business. He felt it was strategic to bring on additional experienced help to manage the workforce. He knew of another Christian business owner, Chris, in the same line of work. Garrett and Chris agreed to co-venture a project with Garrett supplying the job and Chris supplying and managing the workers. As the job progressed Garrett found that Chris' management ability was extremely ineffective. Chris' mismanagement cost them thousands of dollars. Garrett was ultimately responsible for completing the project since the contract was in his name. For the sake of unity with a fellow believer, Garrett forgave Chris and decided not to sue Chris for his negligence. He chose to finish the project at a personal loss. Garrett chose to suffer a personal loss rather than sue a Christian brother. Sometimes unity comes at a very high price.

Behold, how good and how pleasant it is for brothers to dwell together in unity! It is like the precious oil upon the head, coming down upon the beard, even Aaron's beard, coming down upon the edge of his robes. It is like the dew of Hermon coming down upon the mountains of Zion; for there the Lord commanded the blessing—life forever (Psalms 133:1-3).

God places a high value on unity within the body of Christ.

When there is unity, God commands a blessing! Do you want to be blessed? Then strive to build unity on every front. This includes all areas of our lives such as our homes, church, work, friendships and school. Our unity is based on obeying the commandments of Christ with other like-minded believers. There are many passages about unity in the Scripture.

> I do not ask on behalf of these alone, but for those also who believe in Me through their word; that they may all be one; even as You, Father, are in Me and I in You, that they also may be in Us, so that the world may believe that You sent Me (John 17:20-21).

This passage demonstrates the importance of unity. It records Jesus' last hours before being arrested, tortured, and murdered. In the last free moments before His death, He spent time with His Heavenly Father asking that His disciples would be one. In the original language it literally states that He asked that they would be formed into a unit, a team, to carry out God's plan and purposes. Furthering His kingdom should be the basis for our unity with other Christians.

Paul emphasized the importance of being united in one mind and purpose in Philippians 1:27.

> Only conduct yourselves in a manner worthy of the gospel of Christ, so that whether I come and see you or remain absent, I will hear of you that you are standing firm in one spirit, with one mind striving together for the faith of the gospel.

Paul used the word "only" to let us know how important

he considered unity. He also stated that this unity is centered on achieving the goals of Christ: "striving together for the gospel." We are to be united in Christ's purpose for our lives. He rephrased this same command in Philippians 2:2, "make my joy complete by being of the same mind, maintaining the same love, united in spirit, intent on one purpose." This one purpose is to carry Christ's message of reconciliation to the entire world.

> Go therefore and make disciples of all the nations, baptizing them in the name of the Father and the Son and the Holy Spirit, teaching them to observe all that I commanded you; and lo, I am with you always, even to the end of the age (Matthew 28:18-20).

Down through the ages God has always had a purpose for man. Originally, God designed man to rule the Garden of Eden. This was a worthy mission for God's most noble creation. God gave Eve to Adam to be his helper in this endeavor. God's mission for Christians today is a different type of world domination. This mission revolves around spreading the gospel in every nation and making disciples of every person. This immense task requires extreme dedication, ingenuity, vast resources, teamwork, and a focused purpose. We Christians must strive to unite with one another to fulfill God's purpose of furthering His kingdom on earth. As we do this, He can bless us and give us success.

Blessings Come Through Giving

Stephen had been a faithful giver to Christ's work for many years. Then he began to experience financial difficulties. It seemed that nothing was going right for him. He lost his job and had unforeseen expenses. Stephen stopped giving to the Lord's work when his income stopped. When he was finally able to get another job he was really behind financially. So he decided that he would start giving again once he got on his feet. Stephen's circumstances went from bad to worst when he was laid off again. He was unemployed for a few more months. By then he was in dire financial straits. During this time of financial hardship he did not resume his giving. Looking back over the previous months Stephen realized that part of his financial problem may have been related to the fact that he had waited to give to the Lord's work until he was financially secure. Finally one day he was offered a job which would meet his financial needs. He took the job and this time he chose to resume his habit of giving. Over the next decade, God blessed him financially as he remained faithful to give back a portion of his income to the Lord.

> And in everything I showed you that by working hard in this matter you must help the weak and remember the words of the Lord Jesus, that He Himself said, "It is more blessed to give than to receive" (Acts 20:35).

As humans, our nature is to selfishly accumulate riches for ourselves. We are naturally inclined to take, gather, and hoard our resources for our own purposes. We tend to grasp and hold the best for ourselves. In God's economy, the tables are always turned. God says He will bless us if we give to others.

> Honor the Lord from your wealth and from the first of all your produce; so your barns will be filled with plenty and your vats will overflow with new wine. My son, do not reject the discipline of the Lord or loathe His reproof, for whom the Lord loves He reproves.

Even as a father corrects the son in whom he delights (Proverbs 3:9-12).

Do you want God's honor, wealth, and blessings? We need to remember these principles:

1. God gives the power to make wealth.
2. God wants to fill our lives with blessings.
3. If we want God's continued blessing, we must honor Him with our wealth.
4. As we give to God and to others, He can bless us materially.

Impart God's Blessing on Your Children

Then the Lord spoke to Moses, saying, "Speak to Aaron and to his sons, saying, 'Thus you shall bless the sons of Israel. You shall say to them: The Lord bless you, and keep you; The Lord make His face shine on you, and be gracious to you; The Lord lift up His countenance on you and give you peace.' So they shall invoke My name on the sons of Israel, and I then will bless them" (Numbers 6:22-27).

God intended for the Israelites to prosper both materially and spiritually. When this passage was written, the Israelites had just been released after four hundred years of slavery. Their outlook on life was based on oppression, not prosperity. They had no reason to expect success since they had never experienced it. God wanted them to understand that His intention was to make them prosperous. He instituted the command mentioned above—the Israelites were to impart a blessing on their children so they would prosper. The verbal blessing commanded in this passage was from God Himself. He stated that when they invoked the blessing on their children, He would bring it to pass because it was given in His name (Numbers 6:27). The Jews understood the power of this practice. They have continued to practice it to this day and God continues to honor it. Although many Jews today are far from God, He continues to bless them.

Christians should continue this practice of blessing others. You may think this is an Old Testament practice that is out dated for twenty-first century Christians. I must disagree. Jesus demonstrated the power of blessing others. He commanded His followers to "bless those who curse you" (Matthew 5:44). We see the same command repeated by the Apostle Paul. He commands us to "bless those who persecute you, bless and do not curse" (Romans 12:14).

Jesus not only commanded us to bless others, He practiced the habit of giving a verbal blessing. In Mark 10:16, Jesus laid His hands on children and blessed them. When we impart God's blessing on others (such as our children and grandchildren), they prosper as never before.

The Sovereignty of God

Come now, you who say, "Today or tomorrow we will go to such and such a city, and spend a year there and engage in business and make a profit." Yet you do not know what your life will be like tomorrow. You are just a vapor that appears for a little while and then vanishes away. Instead, you ought to say, "If the Lord wills, we will live and do this or that." But as it is, you boast in your arrogance; all such boasting is evil (James 4:13-16).

God has a much bigger purpose for His people than simply to make them wealthy. His driving purpose is to snatch people from hell. He then works to transform their character into the holiness of His Son. God allows trials to happen to us to develop our character and eliminate our weaknesses. He uses circumstances to mold our character. If we will obey His commands, He can ultimately bless us. The Almighty is sovereign. We cannot demand His blessing, but we can ask Him for them. It is God's choice to decide how He will bless us. He not only promises to provide for our needs, sometimes He even pours wealth and riches into our lives. At times He accomplishes these things in unexpected ways. Our Father is the Great Provider who can meet every need and accomplish His purposes. Do not attempt to lower God to the level of your human understanding. Be available to Him and allow Him to bless you in His way.

CHAPTER FIVE

The Four Ingredients of Success

Stuart was very dependable and committed to the Lord. He knew from an early age that he wanted to be self-employed. One thing he lacked was adequate capital to start his own business. He asked God to give him practical direction about how to reach his goal. Over a period of time he decided to save his money and look for a business opportunity which he could pursue. He had a full-time job that was very physically strenuous. He was a diligent, hard worker. The job paid by the amount of work he produced, not by the hour. Because of his high level of production, he was able to earn an above average income. Stuart diligently saved his money. As time passed he discovered a business opportunity in a fast growing high tech industry. He used the money he had saved to open his first business. As demand increased, he opened other offices. Through wisdom, expertise, the development of a plan, and diligence, Stuart's business succeeded. He eventually franchised his business and now it is a national company.

"And by knowledge the rooms are filled with all precious and pleasant riches" (Proverbs 24:4).

"For the Lord gives wisdom; from His mouth come knowledge and understanding. He stores up sound wisdom for the upright; He is a shield to those who walk in integrity" (Proverbs 2:6-7).

"The plans of the diligent lead surely to advantage, but everyone who is hasty comes surely to poverty" (Proverbs 21:5).

"Poor is he who works with a negligent hand, but the hand of the diligent makes rich" (Proverbs 10:4).

These passages show us the four ingredients we need in order to be successful in God's eyes. The first ingredient (as outlined above in Proverbs 24:4) is knowledge. In order to succeed, we must have the knowledge necessary to make wise decisions. Secondly, Proverbs 2:6-7 tells us that we must acquire wisdom. Wisdom is the practical application of knowledge. Proverbs 21:5 tells us not to be hasty about our actions but to diligently plan for success. A plan is the third key ingredient for success. The final passage, Proverbs 10:4, reminds us that the result of laziness is poverty but the result of diligence is wealth. Finally then, we must be diligent to carry out the plans we have made. God has promised great success to those who demonstrate these characteristics.

In summary, these are the four ingredients necessary for true success:

1. You must have knowledge that can be applied practically.
2. You must possess wisdom. Wisdom is the ability to apply the knowledge we gain from experience and from others' advice.
3. You must develop a systematic plan of action.
4. You must be diligent to execute your plan.

So far, we have dealt primarily with matters of the heart. We've discussed the importance of having a right heart and keeping God's purposes in mind when we undertake a task for Him. In the remaining chapters we will discuss specific actions to build wealth in order to fund the work of the Lord. Obviously, there are many specific ways to gain wealth. I do not intend to discuss all the possible avenues to attain riches. Instead, I want to present the principles that are the foundation of wealth and stimulate your creativity so you will be more aware of the opportunities around you.

CHAPTER SIX

Building Wealth Made Practical

Debt

"Owe nothing to anyone except to love one another..."
(Romans 13:8a).

Borrowing is controversial among many Christians. Some say that we should never borrow, that borrowing is wrong and is the result of a sinful life. Some believe we should borrow prudently, expecting the economy to continue to expand. They say we should take advantage of that expansion. They believe that our inflationary spiral, which is common in western developed countries, will continue. I believe we should look to the principles of borrowing in the Scripture to determine our views of this topic.

Romans 13:8 has been used to support the belief that we should never borrow. In order to determine the true meaning of this verse, we will look at its context. We can then draw conclusions that are based on the intent of the writer as demonstrated by verses one through eight.

Every person is to be in subjection to the governing authorities. For there is no authority except from God, and those which exist are established by God. Therefore whoever resists authority has opposed the ordinance of God; and they who have opposed will receive condemnation upon themselves. For rulers are not a cause of fear for good behavior, but for evil. Do you want to have no fear of authority? Do what is good and you will have praise from the same; for it is a minister of God to you for good. But if you do what is evil, be afraid; for it does not bear the sword for nothing; for it is a minister of God, an avenger who brings wrath on the one who practices evil. Therefore it is necessary to be in subjection, not only because of wrath, but also for conscience' sake. For because of this you also pay taxes, for rulers are servants of God, devoting themselves to this very thing. Render to all what is due them: tax to whom tax is due; custom to whom custom; fear to whom fear; honor to whom honor. Owe nothing to anyone except to love one another; for he who loves his neighbor has fulfilled the law.

This passage does not actually focus on debt, it is about the jurisdiction of government. Romans 13:1 states that government is established by God and exists by His authority. Romans 13:2 tells us not to resist authority. The next verse (13:3) cautions us that those who resist authority experience fear and anxiety. From this passage we can understand that God intends for us to live within the laws of government. Verses five through eight bring a conclusion to these instructions.

In Romans 13:5-6, we see that governmental administrators are to be servants of God who are devoted to ruling justly. God established their rule and they have power for our protection. Therefore, we should pay taxes in order to support them and help them do what God has called them to do. Romans 13:7-8 tells us to deliver what is rightfully due to these authorities. This passage is not an injunction against borrowing any money; it is simply a directive to be responsible and pay what is owed.

There are a number of passages in God's word about borrowing. According to my understanding of Scripture, a person should borrow only if he has the ability to repay the loan when it is due, and should only borrow to acquire assets which retain or increase in value. If borrowing is acceptable, the problem arises when we fail to repay what we owe. It is even worse to borrow when you know you do not have the ability to repay. These conclusions are based on several Biblical passages, some of which are discussed below. In the Old Testament, Exodus 22:14 reads,

> If a man borrows anything from his neighbor and it is injured or dies while its owner is not with it, he shall make full restitution.

In other words, if a person borrows something, he is responsible to return it in the same condition or to repay the owner. If God intended to communicate that it is wrong to borrow anything, God would have told the people something like, "Do not borrow." Instead, God told Moses that if you borrow and if whatever you borrow is damaged while in your care; then you should fully restore it. Another example of this principle is found in 2 Kings 6:1-7,

> Now the sons of the prophets said to Elisha, "Behold now, the place before you where we are living is too limited for us. Please let us go to the Jordan and each of us take from there a beam, and let us make a place there for ourselves where we may live." So he said, "Go." Then one said, "Please be willing to go with

your servants." And he answered, "I shall go." So he went with them; and when they came to the Jordan, they cut down trees. But as one was felling a beam, the axe head fell into the water; and he cried out and said, "Alas, my master! For it was borrowed." Then the man of God said, "Where did it fall?" And when he showed him the place, he cut off a stick and threw it in there, and made the iron float. He said, "Take it up for yourself." So he put out his hand and took it.

If you borrow something, it is your responsibility to care for it and to return it. Integrity is the main issue here. Psalms 37:21 gives more insight on the principle of borrowing.

"The wicked borrows and does not pay back, but the righteous is gracious and gives."

God characterized a wicked person as one who borrows but does not repay. Numbers 30:1-2 provides more scriptural support for integrity in borrowing.

Then Moses spoke to the heads of the tribes of the sons of Israel, saying, "This is the word which the Lord has commanded. If a man makes a vow to the Lord, or takes an oath to bind himself with a binding obligation, he shall not violate his word; he shall do according to all that proceeds out of his mouth."

When you borrow, you promise to repay. If you take something that you do not intend to repay, you are not borrowing, but stealing. Stealing is a sin. In contrast then, when we borrow we must repay. Proverbs 22:26-27 tells us,

Do not be among those who give pledges, among those

who become guarantors for debts. If you have nothing with which to pay, why should he take your bed from under you?

Notice that this verse does not say that it is wrong to borrow or to give a pledge. It says "Do not be among those who give pledges…if you have nothing with which to pay." From these verses, we can conclude that it is not a sin to borrow or to give a pledge except when you have no means to repay. Borrowing is a contract, a promise to repay. Of course, we are responsible to be prudent and wise about what we borrow.

When we borrow, we are responsible to repay at the agreed upon terms. For instance, loan payments are calculated as due on regular agreed terms. The payments may be made monthly, quarterly, semi-annually, annually or on any other schedule as determined by contract. The terms of the contract determine when the payment is due. When you borrow, repayment is not due until the agreed upon time. At that time, you are responsible to make that payment. In summary, borrow prudently and repay responsibly. We should only borrow when we know that we have the ability to repay the debt according to the terms of the contract. An additional word of advice that should be considered is that it is prudent to borrow only to acquire assets which retain or increase in value.

During my many years in banking, financial consulting, and personal investments, I have encountered those who have used prudent borrowing to their advantage. As an illustration of one way to apply these principles, let me tell you John's story. Years ago, John was a commercial loan officer at a large bank. He spent most of every day dealing with business people who used credit to increase their assets. One of his customers had acquired many thousands of acres of land over a 20 year period. John asked this man how he was able to acquire this land so readily and then use the acquisitions' rising value to further expand his assets. The customer shared some of his borrowing guidelines with John. John applied these principles to his own circumstances and used debt to increase his assets.

First, John began to save as much money as possible. After saving his money for a few years, he determined that he could make a better income if he were self-employed. John carefully selected a business which allowed him to make the same income as he had made at his bank job while expending 20% less time. Soon he was able to meet his own needs and set aside an additional portion of his money for investment purposes. He then used his free time to look for real estate investment opportunities. Carefully handling his money allowed John to meet his expenses and to have excess money to strategically invest in real estate.

Each year, John set aside money for his investments. He sought knowledge about the real estate development market. John always bought land that lay in the direction toward which the city was growing. He also considered his purchases to be long-term investments. John purchased acreage in blocks of ten, twenty, thirty, or one hundred acres, according to the amount he could repay. The property was always far enough outside urban areas that its cost per acre was relatively low. He particularly favored land intersected by major roads, especially those with timber or mineral rights. John paid at least 50% of the purchase price of the land out of his own capital and borrowed the other half.

He was a responsible borrower and determined how he could service the debt incurred from his cash flow over a five to seven year period. His plan was as follows. As soon as possible, John would sell a corner of his property at a highway intersection for an amount that allowed him to reduce his debt by 25-50%. John then held the land for three to seven years while the city expanded toward it. As the city's growth produced buyers, he would sell the remaining land in smaller parcels. He reduced his debt to zero and earned additional funds which he would save for future investments.

As you can see from this example, when we use debt wisely it can be an effective asset multiplier. Be aware of opportunities to leverage wealth wisely through debt.

Inheritance

Jennifer received a sizeable inheritance that she invested wisely in commercial and residential rental property. Her goal was to buy a few properties every year at below-market prices. She diligently implemented this plan. Now she owns a few hundred rental units worth significantly more than she paid for them. Her inheritance gave her the capital necessary to begin a successful business.

"A good man leaves an inheritance to his children's children, and the wealth of the sinner is stored up for the righteous" (Proverbs 13:22).

God intends for us to leave an inheritance to our descendants so they will have a firm financial beginning. As God provides for His spiritual descendants, so we are to provide for our families. God loves his spiritual family so much that He gave his only begotten Son to redeem them. Earthly families are simply pictures of the spiritual family. When a person receives Christ as his Lord and Savior, that person becomes a son of God (I John 3:1) and a part of the family of God (Ephesians 2:19). Children of God have special privileges and share Christ's inheritance (Galatians 4:7). Just as God has prepared an eternal inheritance for His children, we should provide one for our children. We know that God is very concerned about families. The family is God's basic building block for society. He initiated the family before any other institution including human government or the church. To fully understand the concept of inheritance, we must search for Biblical precedents. God wanted to bless Abraham and his family. In Genesis 15:1-6, we read,

> After these things the word of the Lord came to Abram in a vision, saying, "Do not fear, Abram, I am a shield to you; your reward shall be very great." Abraham said, "Oh Lord God, what will you give to me since I am childless, and the heir of my house is Eliezer of Damascus?" And Abram said, "Since you have given no offspring to me, one born in my house is my heir." Then behold, the word of the Lord came to me saying, "This man will not be your heir; but one who will come forth from your own body, he shall be your heir." And He took him outside and said, "Now look toward the heavens, and count the stars, if you are able to count them." And He said to him, "So shall your descendants be." Then he believed in the Lord; and He reckoned to him as righteousness.

God promised that He would give Abraham a son to be his heir. After this passage Abraham sacrificed a heifer, a goat, a ram, a turtledove and a pigeon and divided them in two. God walked between the pieces and promised to give Abraham with descendants more numerous than the stars of heaven. God intended for Abraham to bless the entire world through his children. In God's time, Abraham and his wife Sarah had a son, Isaac. After

Sarah died, Abraham took another wife and had other children by her. However, when Abraham was about to die, he

"...gave all that he had to Isaac; but to the sons of his concubines Abraham gave gifts while he were still living, and sent them away from his son Isaac eastward, to the land of the east." (Genesis 25:5-6).

Because of the spiritual nature of his relationship with Isaac, Abraham gave a special blessing to him. This blessing was passed down through Isaac to Jacob. Isaac's youngest son, Jacob, received a blessing from his father through deception. Isaac intended to bless his firstborn, Esau, but Jacob deceived Isaac and received the blessing intended for Esau. In Genesis 27:28, Isaac blessed Jacob saying,

Now may God give you the dew of heaven and the of fatness of the earth and an abundance of grain and new wine. May peoples serve you and nations bow down to you. Be master of your brothers and may your mother's sons bow down to you. Cursed be those who curse you and blessed be those who bless you.

God was concerned about Abraham's descendants being prosperous and continuing on the earth, because He planned to bless the entire world through Abraham and his descendants. God blessed these people spiritually and materially. God intended for these men to give an inheritance to their children and even to their grandchildren. During the last days of Jacob's life, God wanted him to bless his sons. By this time, Joseph was already successful and did not need an additional blessing. So Joseph brought his sons to his father for a blessing.

> Now when Israel saw Joseph's sons, he said, "Who are these?" And Joseph said to his father, "They are my sons whom God has given me here." So he said, "Bring them to me, please, that I may bless them." Now the eyes of Israel were so dim from age that he could not see. Then Joseph brought them close to him and he kissed them and embraced them. And Israel said to Joseph, "I never expected to see your face and behold, God has let me see your children as well." Then Joseph took them from his knees and bowed his face to the ground. Then Joseph took them both, Ephraim with his right hand toward Israel's left, and Manasseh with his left hand toward Israel's right, and brought them close to him. But Israel stretched out his right hand and laid it on the head of Ephraim, who was the younger, and his left hand on Manasseh's head, crossing his hands, although Manasseh was first born. He blessed Joseph and said, "The God before whom my fathers Abraham and Isaac walked, the God who has been my Shepherd all my life to this day, the Angel who has redeemed me from all evil, bless the lads; and may my name live on in them, and the names of my fathers Abraham and Isaac; and may they grow into a multitude in the midst of the earth" (Gen. 48:8-16).

Jacob blessed his grandsons because he had a multi-generational view of God's vision in both the spiritual and the material realm. God intends for parents to help their children and grandchildren get a financial advantage in life. This financial head start often makes the difference in whether the family will have a subsistence income level or an abundant level of income. In Genesis chapter 49, Jacob blessed his righteous sons and cursed the sons who were living in sin. He gave an inheritance to his children and his grandchildren, because he wanted them to have a financial foundation for the future so they could accomplish God's will.

In order to accomplish God's will, we must not only know His will and do it, we must also have the material resources needed to accomplish it. Let me give you an example. You may know a person in your church who is struggling financially. She may have an opportunity to take a better job, but she lacks dependable transportation to get to work. God may lead you to help her with her transportation needs by providing a vehicle for her. Without available financial resources, you would not be able to help her. When we bless our descendants with financial resources, we help make it possible for them to bless others.

Self-Employment

Randy was a truck driver who worked for a trucking company for a few years. Randy wanted to be self-employed and began to save money for that venture. Eventually he was able to buy a convenience store which his wife managed. In the meantime, Randy continued to work for the trucking company. After a few more years they sold their store and used the capital to purchase a few trucks. They leveraged their capital through debt to finance part of the equipment. They now have been in the trucking business for about 20 years. They have a fleet of about 150 trucks with revenues exceeding $20 million. They haul goods for companies all over the United States.

"Now Abram was very rich in livestock, in silver and in gold" (Genesis 13:2).

Self-employment is a vehicle which can be very effective for building wealth. Generally speaking, it is easier to build wealth when you are self-employed than when your time must be devoted to making someone else successful. Many self-employed people work in service industries. If you are self-employed and work with a skill you have acquired, you are able to build profit for yourself. There are many examples in the Bible of people who were self-employed. Job, the richest man on earth during his day, was self-employed.

Not only does self-employment allow you the opportunity to gain extra income, it can also allow you to devote more time to your family and to spiritual things. Often when we are employed for other people we lack the flexibility needed to meet these needs.

Self-employment can be a curse or a blessing depending on how you manage it. I have known many self-employed people over the years who have allowed their businesses to dictate their use of time. They have had their lives out-of-balance. God intends for us to be responsible for many important duties in our lives. These include our family, our church, our business and our communities. When a person is self-employed it is easy to allow the business to take an inordinate amount of time, energy, resources and creativity away from other important duties.

Let me give you a personal example of the blessings of self-employment. As I write this, I have two teenagers and three grown children. One summer, two of my older children wanted to explore the possibility of being Christian foreign missionaries. As a self-employed parent with time flexibility, I was able to go with them on mission trip to Europe. We were able to see first hand what it was like to be "in the trenches" ministering to peoples' needs in a foreign land. The experience was very insightful and inspiring for all of us and gave my children a better understanding of this important aspect of the Christian life.

Leverage: Apply What You Have

In Gibeon the Lord appeared to Solomon in a dream at night; and God said, "Ask what you wish me to give you." Then Solomon said, "You have shown great lovingkindness to Your servant David my father, according as he walked before You in truth and righteousness and uprightness of heart toward You; and You have reserved for him this great lovingkindness, that You have given him a son to sit on his throne, as it is this day. Now, O Lord my God, You have made Your servant king in place of my father David, yet I am but a little child; I do not know how to go out or come in. Your servant is in the midst of your people, which You have chosen, a great people who are too many to be numbered or counted. So give Your servant an understanding heart to judge Your people to discern between good and evil. For who is able to judge this great people of Yours?" It was pleasing in the sight of the Lord that Solomon had asked this thing. God said to him, "Because you have asked this thing and have not asked for yourself long life, nor have asked riches for yourself, nor have you asked for the life of your enemies, but have asked for yourself discernment to understand justice, behold, I have done according to your words. Behold, I have given you a wise and discerning heart, so that there has been no one like you before you, nor shall one like you arise after you. I have also given you what you have not asked, both riches and honor, so that there will not be any among the kings like you all your days" (1 Kings 3:5-13).

Leverage is the effective use of a tool to help you achieve greater results with less effort. Leverage is developed through the effective use of three basic resources: manpower, capital and technology. Once you have God's wisdom and insight into how to develop wealth along with a plan of action and the diligence to carry it out, you still must employ these three resources in order to succeed. As our primary example, we will see how King Solomon effectively used all three of these resources to build a fortune.

Employ Manpower

Solomon used manpower in two ways. First, he appointed managers and held them accountable. Secondly, he mobilized and managed a skilled workforce. On a side note, the Biblical passage above also exemplifies the need for God's wisdom and knowledge. Solomon had both wisdom and knowledge and he immediately put them into action.

His first effective use of his manpower was to appoint managers.

Now King Solomon was king over all Israel. These were his officials: Azariah the son of Zadok was the priest; Elihoreph and Ahijah, the sons of Shisha were secretaries; Jehoshaphat the son of Ahilud was the recorder; and Benaiah the son of Jehoiada was over the army;

and Zadok and Abiathar were priests; and Azariah the son of Nathan was over the deputies; and Zabud the son of Nathan, a priest, was the king's friend; and Ahishar was over the household; and Adoniram the son of Abda was over the men subject to forced labor. Solomon had twelve deputies over all Israel, who provided for the king and his household; each man had to provide for a month in the year. These are their names: Ben-hur, in the hill country of Ephraim; Ben-deker in Makaz and Shaalbim and Beth-shemesh and Elon-beth-hanan; Ben-hesed, in Arubboth (Socoh was his and all the land of Hepher); Ben-abinadab, in all the height of Dor (Taphath the daughter of Solomon was his wife); Baana the son of Ahilud, in Taanach and Megiddo, and all Beth-shean which is beside Zarethan below Jezreel, from Beth-shean to Abel-meholah as far as the other side of Jokmeam; Ben-geber, in Ramoth-gilead (the towns of Jair, the son of Manasseh, which are in Gilead were his: the region of Argob, which is in Bashan, sixty great cities with walls and bronze bars were his); Ahinadab the son of Iddo, in Mahanaim; Ahimaaz, in Naphtali (he also married Basemath the daughter of Solomon); Baana the son of Hushai, in Asher and Bealoth; Jehoshaphat the son of Paruah, in Issachar; Shimei the son of Ela, in Benjamin; Geber the son of Uri, in the land of Gilead, the country of Sihon king of the Amorites and of Og king of Bashan; and he was the only deputy who was in the land (I Kings 4:1-9).

These verses list the men Solomon appointed to help him manage his kingdom. I've included this entire passage because I want you to see the extent of Solomon's government. Solomon's decision to appoint managers was extremely wise and productive. His first advisors were spiritual advisors (verse I). In I Kings 4:3, we see that he had secretaries and recorders who ensured that all policies and practices he initiated were recorded properly. He also had a commander over his army. Many kings in his day were actually involved in leading their armies. However, being commander of an army was a full-time job. Solomon chose to delegate that important job to a faithful, trust-worthy man. He also had a supervisor over the twelve deputies whom he appointed to rule Israel. The deputies administered the laws of the kingdom and provided the provisions to run the government.

By appointing effective managers who relieved him of the everyday duties of government, Solomon was free to focus his attention on providing visionary leadership to his nation. Solomon knew that it was vital to have a skilled workforce to accomplish his plans.

> Now Hiram king of Tyre sent his servants to Solomon, when he heard that they had anointed him king in place of his father, for Hiram had always been a friend of David. Then Solomon sent word to Hiram, saying, "You know that David my father was unable to build a house for the name of the LORD his God because of the wars which surrounded him, until the LORD put them under the soles of his feet. But now the LORD my God has given me rest on every side; there is neither adversary nor misfortune. Behold, I intend to build a house for the name of the LORD my God, as the LORD spoke to David my father, saying, 'Your son, whom I will set on your throne in your place, he will build the house for My name.' Now

therefore, command that they cut for me cedars from Lebanon, and my servants will be with your servants; and I will give you wages for your servants according to all that you say, for you know that there is no one among us who knows how to cut timber like the Sidonians." When Hiram heard the words of Solomon, he rejoiced greatly and said, "Blessed be the LORD today, who has given to David a wise son over this great people." So Hiram sent word to Solomon, saying, "I have heard the message which you have sent me; I will do what you desire concerning the cedar and cypress timber. My servants will bring them down from Lebanon to the sea; and I will make them into rafts to go by sea to the place where you direct me, and I will have them broken up there, and you shall carry them away. Then you shall accomplish my desire by giving food to my household." So Hiram gave Solomon as much as he desired of the cedar and cypress timber. Solomon then gave Hiram 20,000 kors of wheat as food for his household, and twenty kors of beaten oil; thus Solomon would give Hiram year by year. The LORD gave wisdom to Solomon, just as He promised him; and there was peace between Hiram and Solomon, and the two of them made a covenant. Now King Solomon levied forced laborers from all Israel; and the forced laborers numbered 30,000 men. He sent them to Lebanon, 10,000 a month in relays; they were in Lebanon a month and two months at home. And Adoniram was over the forced laborers. Now Solomon had 70,000 transporters and 80,000 hewers of stone in the mountains, besides Solomon's 3,300 chief deputies who were over the project and who ruled over the people who were doing the work. Then the king commanded, and they quarried great stones, costly stones, to lay the foundation of the house with cut stones. So Solomon's builders and Hiram's builders and the Gebalites cut them, and prepared the timbers and the stones to build the house.

Solomon's use of a skilled workforce is recorded in I Kings 5:1-18. In this passage we find Hiram, the king of Tyre, was a loyal friend to Solomon's father David. Hiram sent Solomon a greeting when Solomon became king and the two kings made an alliance. Solomon told Hiram that David had appointed Solomon to build the house of the Lord. Solomon stated that he intended to build a house for the Lord God. He asked Hiram to command that cedars be cut from Lebanon. Solomon assured Hiram that he would pay Hiram's servants for this work. He requested that Hiram's men work with Israel's workforce. Solomon honored Hiram and said that there was no one among Israel who knew how to cut timber like Hiram's men.

From these passages, we observe that Solomon understood the value of having an effective workforce. He also knew how to motivate people to be productive. Solomon was a great king with a strong and effective standing army. He could have simply conquered the entire region and taken the timbers by force. Solomon knew that he could accomplish his purpose more effectively through persuasion and diplomacy.

Solomon was conscious of the physical constraints of his workers. He utilized a shift rotation model to successfully complete his task. In First Kings 5:13, he levied a workforce of 30,000 men from Israel. Each month he sent a different group of 10,000 men in relays to Lebanon. They were in Lebanon for one month and home for two months. In addition to these men, Solomon had a workforce of 70,000 transporters who were responsible to move the logs from Lebanon to Jerusalem. From this passage we understand that—when it is used correctly—a skillful and motivated workforce can accomplish extraordinary things.

Utilize Capital

The second element of leverage is capital. God provided the capital that Solomon needed in three ways:

I. His father, King David, left him a significant inheritance so he had capital available for immediate use.

> Now Solomon ruled over all the kingdoms from the River to the land of the Philistines and to the border of Egypt; they brought tribute and served Solomon all the days of his life. Solomon's provision for one day was thirty kors of fine flour and sixty kors of meal, ten fat oxen, twenty pasture-fed oxen, a hundred sheep besides deer, gazelles, roebucks, and fattened fowl. For he had dominion over everything west of the River, from Tiphsah even to Gaza, over all the kings west of the River; and he had peace on all sides around about him. So Judah and Israel lived in safety, every man under his vine and his fig tree, from Dan even to Beersheba, all the days of Solomon. Solomon had 40,000 stalls of horses for his chariots, and 12,000 horsemen. Those deputies provided for King Solomon and all who came to King Solomon's table, each in his month; they left nothing lacking. They also brought barley and straw for the horses and swift steeds to the place where it should be, each according to his charge (I Kings 4:21-28).

2. Solomon had the ability to raise revenues through taxing Israel and the other nations subject to him. He raised taxes effectively yet not oppressively. The people were prosperous under his rule, although he did not use his power wisely toward the end of his life.

> For the king had at sea the ships of Tarshish with the ships of Hiram; once every three years the ships of Tarshish came bringing gold and silver, ivory and apes and peacocks. So King Solomon became greater than all the kings of the earth in riches and in wisdom. All the earth was seeking the presence of Solomon, to hear his wisdom which God had put in his heart. They brought every man his gift, articles of silver and gold, garments, weapons, spices, horses, and mules, so much year by year. Now Solomon gathered chariots and horsemen; and he had 1,400 chariots and 12,000 horsemen, and he stationed them in the chariot cities and with the king in Jerusalem. The king made silver as common as stones in Jerusalem, and he made cedars as plentiful as sycamore trees that are in the lowland. Also Solomon's import of horses was from Egypt and Kue, and the king's merchants procured them from Kue for a price (I Kings 10:22-28).

3. Solomon was a very wealthy man. He knew how to generate more wealth through private enterprise. He made significant investments in land, infrastructure, natural resources, commodities and transportation. Since he was a diversified investor, he was not dependent on one sector of the economy.

"When Hiram heard the words of Solomon, he rejoiced

greatly and said, 'Blessed be the LORD today, who has given to David a wise son over this great people'" (I Kings 5:7).

Harness Technology

The third element of leverage is technology. Solomon used the cutting edge technology of his day to accomplish extraordinary tasks. He utilized transporters for the large stones used to build the temple, his palaces, and public structures. Solomon implemented advanced mechanical techniques to effectively transport a substantial quantity of extremely weighty and cumbersome building materials. In addition to the advanced use of mechanical advantage, Solomon set up a network of roads in order to transport these materials. He used capital to secure vast caches of natural resources such as timber. He then used technology to change this raw material into a finished product. Today we would call that a value-added product.

> Then the king commanded, and they quarried great stones, costly stones, to lay the foundation of the house with cut stones. So Solomon's builders and Hiram's builders and the Gebalites cut them, and prepared the timbers and the stones to build the house (I Kings 5:17-18).

"The foundation was of costly stones, even large stones, stones of ten cubits and stones of eight cubits" (I Kings 7:10).

Technology was a very important aspect of these projects. Solomon understood that technology and manpower go hand-in-hand. Technology is only effective when used by a trained workforce. Solomon needed a trained workforce to accomplish these gigantic tasks. For your reference, I Kings 6 gives more information about this workforce and the building of the temple. The temple was a huge and intricate structure. It had very specific designs and the technology used to build it was state-of-the-art. All the walls and the ceiling were made of cedar and the floors were made of cypress wood. Solomon completely covered the ceilings, walls, and floors of the temple with gold. Obviously that was extremely costly. Solomon must have had virtually unlimited capital. He also had advanced knowledge of metallurgy technology and the ability to fashion gold. The gold was molded into sheets which would have been very heavy and cumbersome. It was to be fastened to the wood without marring the surface of the gold. This would require fasteners on the back of the gold sturdy enough to hold the gold and designed to conceal the attachment. Even now, with our modern technology, it is difficult to get buildings plumb and true. They were able to complete the project even while using rough cedar and cypress as their subsurface material.

Much of the wood in the temple was artistically carved. I Kings 6:4 says that the house had windows with artistic frames. The doorposts on the west side and on the right side of the chamber were very elaborate. I Kings 6:18 states that the cedar inside the house was carved into the shapes of gourds and open flowers and no stone could be seen. Inside the inner sanctuary they built two cherubim of olive wood, each ten cubits high (I Kings 6:22-23). Each cherub had two wings, each of which was 7.5 feet tall. This gigantic work of art was very delicately crafted. Solomon had all the walls in the house carved with engravings. A project of this scope required advanced engineering technology. We build many types of intricate projects today with machines. In his century, Solomon was able to accomplish these identical works of art without laser driven technology.

In addition to the building of the temple, I Kings 7 states

that Solomon built his own palace in thirteen years. Like the temple, it was made of cedar inside with artistic windows and frames. His palace had a large porch that was 75 feet long and 45 feet wide. The porch was lined with immense pillars. Imagine how difficult it must have been to raise those pillars without cranes or other modern hydraulic technology. The foundation of Solomon's palace was large, costly stones. In our modern times we have bulldozers, trucks, and cranes. He and his workforce had a very clear understanding of mechanical advantage in order to move these massive objects. Beyond that, he also had the technological ability to do very intricate work.

As recorded in I Kings 7:15-22, Solomon commissioned Hiram of Tyre to build two bronze pillars for the temple. Each was twenty-seven feet tall and eighteen feet in circumference. Each pillar had a 7.5 foot tall ornamental decoration on top which was called a capital. These capitals were decorated with a lattice work and interwoven chains. On top of the capitals were two rows of bronze pomegranates. Today, Hiram of Tyre would be considered a skilled metallurgist.

Solomon and his workers understood the laws of geometry, trigonometry and physics. In addition to these projects, Solomon did many other projects which are summarized in Ecclesiastes,

> I enlarged my works: I built houses for myself, I planted vineyards for myself; I made gardens and parks for myself and I planted in them all kinds of fruit trees; I made ponds of water for myself from which to irrigate a forest of growing trees. I bought male and female slaves and I had homeborn slaves. Also I possessed flocks and herds larger than all who preceded me in Jerusalem. Also, I collected for myself silver and gold and the treasure of kings and provinces. I provided for

myself male and female singers and the pleasures of men—many concubines. Then I became great and increased more than all who preceded me in Jerusalem. My wisdom also stood by me (Ecclesiastes 2:4-9).

As you can see, technology and a trained workforce are intricately connected, because you can not use technology effectively without a qualified workforce. Solomon became rich and powerful through the effective use of these principles. First of all, he was extremely wise. I Kings 4:32-34 states,

He also spoke 3000 proverbs, and his songs were 1005. He spoke of trees, from the cedar that is in Lebanon even to the hyssop that grows on the wall; he spoke also of animals and birds and creeping things and fish. Men came from all peoples to hear the wisdom of Solomon, from all the kings of the earth who had heard of his wisdoms.

He took all the wisdom, knowledge, and insight God had given him and developed a plan for success. He was diligent to accomplish each plan. Then he used his wisdom to motivate others to facilitate his plan. He appointed managers and held them accountable. He empowered them to accomplish these things. He both developed plans and accomplished them. God richly blessed him until he became great and was wealthier than anyone else on the earth. Solomon had many different projects, including construction, farming, vineyards, and gardens, and parks. He researched different types of plants and fruit trees. He experimented with irrigation and with water resources. He had livestock and herds of animals. Solomon must have determined what produced the strongest types of livestock and used that knowledge successfully. He had brilliant insight and a vast knowledge base to use to multiply his wealth. Solomon understood technology and used it to his advantage. Solomon became wealthy through the effective use of manpower, capital and technology.

Capital Investments

As we gather knowledge from God, expertise from our own experience, and wisdom from the success and failures of others, we are able to make a plan for success. Then we must be diligent to carry out that plan while utilizing manpower, capital and technology. In this section, we will apply these principles to investments. There are many types of opportunities in which to invest your resources. If someone found an investment that yielded a 20-50% annual return, he would probably believe that it was too good to be true. Most investments yield a much smaller return. The following Scriptural example of Isaac shows how God can bless abundantly beyond our prayers and hopes.

> Now Isaac sowed in the land and reaped in the same year a hundredfold. And the Lord blessed him, and the man became rich, and continued to grow richer until he became very wealthy; for he had possessions of flocks and herds and a great household, so that the Philistines envied him (Genesis 26:12-14).

Isaac sought God, meditated on God's word, believed the promises of God, and gathered knowledge and wisdom. Isaac was trained by his father, Abraham, in horticulture, agriculture, and animal husbandry. He had all the ingredients for success. He possessed capital in the form of land and herds. He had knowledge and wisdom about many topics. He had a large, experienced workforce. He developed a plan and he sought God. Most importantly, he had the favor of God because of the way he lived. This passage tells us that God blessed Isaac. You can have all the ingredients for success, but if you are not blessed by God, you will not acquire true riches. I know people who have all the necessary ingredients except for a right heart. They are not seeking God so God cannot bless them. In fact, they are cursed by Him and their wealth is given to others because of their wickedness. God richly blessed Isaac because Isaac put his trust in the Living God. Chapter 26 of Genesis tells us that in one year God blessed Isaac a hundred-fold. Think about that literally. Imagine investing $20,000 and receiving a return of $2,000,000 in one year! That is the equivalent of Isaac's experience. As a result of Isaac's obedience to God's principles, God blessed him and made him a very wealthy man.

John Rockefeller, an American entrepreneur of the 1800's, understood the principles of building wealth through capital investments. He understood that because of the growing economy and the invention of the automobile, America would have an increasing need for gasoline. Rockefeller chose to focus all his resources on securing oil and gas producing properties, refineries, and a distribution network. The refineries would be used to change the raw material to usable products. Of course, we would call this process adding value. The distribution network that he developed delivered those products to his target market. Rockefeller understood the concept of using manpower, capital and technology to expand his investments. Using the principles discussed throughout this book, Rockefeller experienced amazing success. His business expanded until the government believed it was too large and ordered that it be divided. As a result of Rockefeller's efforts, he became very wealthy. John Rockefeller's vision was to leave an inheritance to his heirs. You can trace his family tree and find that many of his great-great grandchildren still have significant wealth because of his efforts.

These ideas have been successfully implemented many times throughout American history. In the 19th century, Andrew Carnegie realized that the boom in construction would continue throughout the 19th and 20th centuries. He invested his capital into iron ore fields and steel mills. His efforts paid off phenomenally and he became a wealthy man. Carnegie was generous with his wealth and endowed charities across the country.

In the 1950's, Ray Kroc saw that America wanted convenience. He set up a chain of fast food restaurants known as McDonalds. The fast food franchise was born from his model. Kroc's franchise now stretches across the globe. Now many of our children do not remember life without McDonald's.

Other entrepreneurs understood the value of land and timber. They acquired land with timber and built factories to produce lumber and other wood products. These men and women have found success in producing wood-based products such as paper, plywood, medium-density fiberboard, and even the finished products: furniture, millwork, doors, windows, and other products too numerous to mention.

In order to be successful, a person must have practical knowledge, a plan, and wisdom to know how to implement that plan. They must have diligence to carry out their plan. These qualities are extremely valuable for a person who has capital and utilizes both manpower and technology to take advantage of their opportunities. We have seen multiple examples of successful investors throughout history. Now I want you to understand that successful capital investing is not a thing of the past. I want you to realize the incredible number of opportunities for success in today's world. I am going to give you a few practical examples of opportunities for successful investing, but realize that the opportunities are virtually unlimited. Through a diligent search you can find many other investment opportunities. You may find it worthwhile to work closely with mentors who are willing to share their "secrets" and advice with you. Finding a mentor is often very helpful to a person who wants to expand their knowledge and opportunities.

The first practical investment opportunity I would like to share with you is in the technological industry. The Internet as we know it has only been in use for a short time, but its global effect on the way we do business is phenomenal. Today if you do not have an Internet presence, you may not be able to succeed in business. The Internet industry is still young. It offers many business opportunities in all areas that support the Internet, especially technology and technology-related business services.

Another area of opportunity for productive capital investment is to export the goods and services that we enjoy in the West to the emerging third-world countries. For instance, China has an almost insatiable urge for vehicles, electronics and other products. There are fortunes to be made for those whose faith and diligence has empowered them to take advantage of these opportunities.

When you have expertise in any specific area, you will be able to see investment opportunities in that field. There are capital investments available in practically every field. Some specific areas of opportunity include: medicine, real estate, health care, and financial services. I encourage you to look for opportunities—in your field of expertise—to build your assets through the principles we have discussed.

CHAPTER SEVEN

Twelve Steps to Wealth

In the earlier sections, we have discussed the importance of developing the ability to earn an income to:
1. Support yourself and your family.
2. Give to the cause of Christ.
3. Save for expected needs and investments.
4. Invest to build wealth.

This chapter will discuss practical steps to build riches in order to reach those goals. These twelve steps include practical advice for a wide age range. In order to make the advice more applicable to you, I have divided the twelve steps into two sections. This chapter is directed toward two groups of people. The first section is tailored for people aged thirty and younger. The second section is directed toward people over age thirty. These groupings are intended to direct your attention to advice that is pertinent for you. However, you will find value in reading and understanding this entire chapter. For example, if you are in the older group, the section for younger people may point out some areas you neglected in earlier years and help you formulate a plan to restore what is missing in your financial development. If you are younger, knowing what to focus on now and later in life will help you be content in your formative financial years.

Advice for Young People

1. Learn to walk with Christ and be pleasing to Him at an early age.

"But seek first His kingdom and His righteousness, and all these things will be added to you" (Matthew 6:33).

Matthew 6:33 encourages each of us to learn early in life to put Christ first. Even children can be taught to employ this principle successfully. Colossians 3:20 addresses children,

"Children, be obedient to your parents in all things, for this is well pleasing to the Lord."

Young people should develop habits that lead to success as soon as possible. God can be pleased with a young person as much as He can be pleased with an adult who has known God for many years. God can use young and older people alike as they yield their wills to His perfect will. Take God's value system into your heart and life and put it into action. Paul, the apostle, encouraged Timothy, a young person, to "let no one look down on your youthfulness, but rather in speech, conduct, love, faith and purity, show yourself an example to those who believe" (I Timothy 4:12.)

2. Develop a strong work ethic while you are young. Proverbs 20:11 tells us that "It is by his deeds that a lad distinguishes himself, if his conduct is pure and right."

In order to achieve success, a person must acquire a skill, an education, and a solid work ethic. It is better to finance education through scholarships, work study programs or grants rather than through debt.

"Do you see a man skilled in his work, he will stand before kings. He will not stand before obscure men" (Proverbs 22:29).

Possessing a marketable skill is vital to the process of accumulating riches. There is an incredible difference in the amount of income that can be accumulated over the years by simply starting early. Education is important, and I definitely do not want to de-emphasize it, but whatever education you have must be geared toward a practical way to earn income. Your marketable skill does not have to be an ability intended for your sole support for the rest of your life. It may be a skill that you can learn in six months to a year. When you start, you may be making minimum wage, but with marketable skill you may can double your hourly wage. Develop a marketable skill as quickly as you can and implement it to acquire the resources that you need.

3. Before we can invest, we must satisfy the basic needs of food, shelter, and clothing. Often, we believe that "necessities" go beyond these basic resources. The Apostle Paul wrote, "If we have food and covering, with these we shall be content" (I Timothy 6:8).

Contentment is a precious gift. The Scriptures say we should be content with just the basics: food, covering, shelter. Here in America, we have swallowed the lie that we must have designer clothes, an expensive home, a new vehicle, and many other things in order to be valuable. God says that we are valuable simply because He gave His Son to die for us. In His eyes, our value is not determined by what we own. As you develop your resources, do not buy too far beyond your basic needs. Our society motivates us to have newer, bigger, better things: cars, homes and status toys. We sometimes feel that we can not be content without more stuff. God wants us to be content with the basics: food, clothing, shelter, and His love.

> Make sure that your character is free from the love of money, being content with what you have. For He Himself has said, "I will never desert you nor will I

ever forsake you so that we confidently say, 'The Lord is my helper, I will not be afraid. What will man do to me?'" (Hebrews 13:5).

4. Save to acquire tools to do your job effectively and to have funds to invest. For most Americans, saving has become a lost art that begs to be reinstated. During my years as a banker, I learned that surprisingly few people put money into savings. In my observation, the percentage of our population who save has steadily declined in the last thirty years. Whether our savings is a dollar or ten thousand dollars, each of us can save some part of what we earn. Savings is a long-term project as illustrated in the next passage. The earlier we start saving, the more likely we are to achieve the greatest rewards.

In Genesis chapters twenty-seven through thirty-one we find an interesting account of a man who gained great wealth by saving for a long period of time. Jacob tricked his father and received the blessing that should have gone to his older brother, Esau. Esau became furious and wanted to kill Jacob. Jacob had to flee for his life. His mother sent him to her brother, Laban. There Jacob met Laban's daughter Rachel and fell in love with her. He made an agreement with Laban that he would work for Laban for seven years and then receive Rachel as his wife. However, Jacob's deceitfulness was returned to him. Laban tricked him and gave him Rachel's sister, Leah as a bride. When Jacob discovered his father-in-law's deceit, Laban promised Rachel to him as a second wife, but Laban required that Jacob work for another seven years for Rachel. According to Genesis 31:38, this story takes place over a twenty year period. Jacob repented of his sin and worked very hard during this twenty year period. God transformed his character during this difficult time in his life. At the end of the first 14 years, Jacob became Laban's partner and God richly blessed him financially. At the end of the 20 years, Jacob was ready to go back home and be reconciled to his brother. Jacob and his family stole away in the middle of the night, because he was afraid that Laban would not allow him to leave. When Laban realized that Jacob was gone, he tracked him down. The following passage records Jacob's words to Laban.

> These twenty years I have been with you; your ewes and your female goats have not miscarried, nor have I eaten the rams of your flocks. That which was torn of beasts I did not bring to you; I bore the loss of it myself. You required it of my hand whether stolen by day or stolen by night. Thus I was: by day the heat consumed me and the frost by night, and my sleep fled from my eyes. These twenty years I have been in your house; I served you fourteen years for your two daughters and six years for your flock, and you changed my wages ten times. If the God of my father, the God of Abraham and the fear of Isaac, had not been for me, surely now you would have sent me away empty-handed. God has seen my affliction and the toil of my hands, so He rendered judgment last night. (Genesis 31:38-42).

This passage illustrates my point that earning wealth usually takes place over long period of time. We should not expect it to come overnight. God will bless our lives when we are consistently faithful to work diligently for Him.

5. Select a spouse who shares your values, goals and objectives. "Can two walk together, except they be agreed?" (Amos 3:3) (KJV).

Today we often select our mate based on many superficial things, such as the way they look, talk or laugh. Some people base their qualifications for a mate strictly on physical or sexual attraction. God wants us to choose a mate based on His value system. More practical advice on this topic is found in the next passage.

> Do not be bound together with unbelievers; for what partnership has righteousness and lawlessness, or what fellowship has light with darkness? Or what harmony has Christ with Belial, or what has a believer in common with an unbeliever? Or what agreement has the temple of God with idols? For we are the temple of the living God, just as God said, "I will dwell among them and walk among them; and I will be their God, and they will be My people. Therefore, come out from their midst and be separate," says the Lord; "And do not touch any unclean thing; and I will welcome you. And I will be a Father to you, and you will be sons and daughters to Me, says the Lord Almighty" (2 Corinthians 6:14-18).

The very first prerequisite for a mate is that they should be a mature Christian. They definitely should have trusted Christ and at least learned the basics of the Christian life. It is important that they have a history of pleasing God, walking with Him, reaching others, and developing godly character. If you are single, consider these qualifications in your search for a mate. If you have children who are in the process of selecting a mate, encourage them to follow these guidelines. If you are married to someone who is not a Christian or who is a carnal Christian, set aside the idea of accumulating wealth and focus your attention on helping your spouse grow in their relationship with Christ. Focus on helping them develop into the kind of person God wants them to be. If you are in that circumstance, the development of your spouse's character is much more important than accumulating wealth.

Advice for Older People

6. Develop the habit of giving. In the Old Testament, God required that the Israelites pay one tenth of their income as a tithe. In addition to that, they had the opportunity to give an offering. In the Old Testament, we see the giving of tithes and offerings. In the New Testament, we are not commanded to give a tithe. Instead we see that God expects the Christian to make all his assets available to the Lord. This is demonstrated in 2 Corinthians 8:1-12.

> Now, brethren, we wish to make known to you the grace of God which has been given to the churches of Macedonia, that in a great ordeal of affliction their abundance of joy and their deep poverty overflowed in the wealth of their liberality. For I testify that according to their ability, and beyond their ability, they gave of their own accord, begging us with much urging for the favor of participation in the support of the saints, and this, not as we had expected, but they first gave themselves to the Lord and to us by the will of God. So we urged Titus that as he had previously made a beginning, so he would also complete in you this gracious work as well. But just as you abound in everything, in faith and utterance and knowledge and in all earnestness and in the love we inspired in you, see

that you abound in this gracious work also. I am not speaking this as a command, but as proving through the earnestness of others the sincerity of your love also (2 Corinthians 8:1-8).

In this passage, Paul encouraged the Corinthians to give in order to supply the needs of the saints in Judea. There was a famine in Judea at that time, and the Christians in the other parts of the world felt responsible to help their Christian brothers and sisters. The Corinthians had promised to send a gift to the believers in Judea. Paul was visiting all the churches and collecting money for the relief effort. In this passage, Paul used Macedonians as an example of sacrificial giving. The Macedonians were very poor people, but they had big hearts. They wanted to share in God's work. Indeed, the Macedonians were actually in a difficult financial situation, but God laid it on their hearts to give. Paul used them as an example to show the Corinthians how important it is to give.

The principle of giving is also illustrated in the next chapter of Second Corinthians:

Now this I say, he who sows sparingly will also reap sparingly, and he who sows bountifully will also reap bountifully. Each one must do just as he has purposed in his heart, not grudgingly or under compulsion, for God loves a cheerful giver. And God is able to make all grace abound to you, so that always having all sufficiency in everything, you may have an abundance for every good deed; as it is written, "He scattered abroad, he gave to the poor, his righteousness endures forever." Now He who supplies seed to the sower and bread for food will supply and multiply your seed for sowing and increase the harvest of your righteousness; you will be enriched in everything for all liberality, which through us is producing thanksgiving to God (2 Corinthians 9:6-11.

Though not explicitly required in the New Testament, developing a habit of giving tithes and offerings fulfills God's plan for Christians to give of their assets to advance the kingdom of God. In fact, Psalms 24:1 tells us that *everything* belongs to the Lord.

"The earth is the Lord's, and all it contains, the world, and all those who dwell in it." (Psalm 24:1)

Although it is God's plan for Christian to give, He wants us to be discerning when we give. We are not to give randomly to any "ministry." Instead, we should attempt to give to people or ministries who have a legitimate need and Godly purpose. For instance, in I Timothy 5:17-18 Paul tells us:

The elders who rule well are to be considered worthy of double honor, especially those who work hard at preaching and teaching. For the Scripture says, "You shall not muzzle the ox while he is threshing," and "the laborer is worthy of his wages."

In these two verses it is obvious that the spiritual leaders who are effective in teaching and preaching the Word of God, should be compensated financially. This is merely one example of effective giving. It is an extremely important that Christians develop a habit of giving. We are blessed through our giving. Jesus said, "It is more blessed to give than to receive" (Acts 20:35b).

7. Invest your savings wisely, systematically, and with diversity. It is important for you to develop your own criteria and guidelines for managing your risk. If you can not sleep at night because you are worrying about your investment, it is probably better to invest in some other way. Evaluate the success of your investments regularly. If your plan is not working, alter it. It is important for you to be systematic and consistent over a long period of time.

Once you begin to have success with investments, you may face a new set of temptations. For instance, success in investing can lead to foolish spending. When we have additional money, we may be tempted to spend it on extravagant and nonessential items. I recommend that you be temperate in your spending. This principle is illustrated to some extent in the convenience industry. For example, fast food initially looks like a time saver, but most of the time it is a waste of our resources. When we are in a bind because we have not properly used our time or because we have over committed ourselves, we may feel that we are justified to stop at a fast food restaurant. I am not saying that we should never eat fast food; however, I think that it should be the exception, rather than the norm.

8. Borrow responsibly and always be mindful to repay the debt incurred. If you borrow, do it to acquire assets that will retain their value or increase in value. I do not recommend borrowing for an education or for consumer goods such as boats, cars, or any entertainment items for recreation. Always remember that all we have belongs to God. Wisely use the resources He has provided to you.

9. Plan for the future. God intends for you to leave an inheritance for your children and grandchildren. You can influ-

ence the spiritual and physical welfare of your children, grand-children, and even great-grandchildren. Implement a plan to give them part of an inheritance at strategic milestones in their lives such as when they graduate from school, marry, buy a home, and/or start a business. In Luke 15, the prodigal son asked his father for his share of the inheritance. The father did not seem to think it was an unusual request to give an inheritance before he died. It was normal to give a portion of an inheritance so that one's son could start a new life with a family of his own. Finally, provide a significant portion of your children's inheritance to them at your death. If possible, provide an inheritance for the next generation, too. Teach your children to plan to give an inheritance to their children and grandchildren as well.

10. Seek to become self-employed if it is possible.

> Were you called while a slave? Do not worry about it. But if you are able also to become free, rather do that. For he who was called in the Lord while a slave is the Lord's freedman; likewise he who was called while free is Christ's slave. You were bought at a price; do not become slaves of men (1 Corinthians 7:21-23).

The principle in I Corinthians 7:21-23 is that if you can become free, do so. If you cannot, do not worry about it. Slavery is not an issue today as it was in the first century. I believe that in modern times, this verse applies to self-employment. In other words, if you are employed and you can become free—be your own boss and make your own decisions—it is better to do that. Then you are more flexible and available to God. God is then able to bless you and your business directly. Abraham was a self-employed herdsman with an understanding of horticulture and agriculture. God blessed him through self-employment. "Abram was very rich in livestock, silver, and gold." (Genesis 13:2) As the richest man in his day, Job was self-employed. Finally, Solomon, the richest man who ever lived, was also self-employed. Through these examples we see that men can build great wealth through self-employment—when God blesses them.

11. Learn to employ the three universal tools of the leverage principle: manpower, capital and technology. These three tools are essential when building wealth. Although these principles are universal, you must customize them for the profession you choose and to the type of investments you make. Ask God for specific instruction about how you should apply the principles of leverage. Also, seek advice from mentors and experts in your field.

12. Lastly, we must understand there are two ways to acquire and accumulate wealth. One way is through entrepreneurship. This is the way Bill Gates built Microsoft and Sam Walton built Wal-mart. Building significant wealth this way is very difficult and requires a very gifted individual. In comparison, there are huge numbers of people who have utilized the second way of accumulating wealth: prudent investing of capital. The great Biblical example of this way of wealth accumulation is the story of how God blessed Isaac with a hundred-fold return on his invested crops in one year (Genesis 26:12-15).

CHAPTER EIGHT

The Gift of Giving

Now Joseph, a Levite of Cyprian birth, who was also called Barnabas by the apostles (which translated means "son of encouragement"), and who owned a tract of land, sold it and brought the money and laid it at the apostles' feet (Acts 4:36-37).

People with sharing hearts have always been an important part of the Christian church. Barnabas was such a man. He made his assets available to Christ's cause and then devoted his life to spreading the good news of the Kingdom of God.

Among the gifts of the Spirit listed in Romans 12:6-8 we find the gift of giving. Paul said that people who have the gift of giving should exercise it liberally.

Since we have gifts that differ according to the grace given to us, each of us is to exercise them accordingly: if prophecy, according to the proportion of his faith; if service, in his serving; or he who teaches, in his teaching; or he who exhorts, in his exhortation; he who gives with liberality; he who leads, with diligence; he who shows mercy, with cheerfulness (Romans 12:6-8).

People with the gift of giving often have the ability to accumulate wealth, as well. If you have this gift, I would encourage you to devote yourself to giving and make that a big part of your personal ministry. In I Timothy 6:17b-18, Paul instructs those who are rich in this present world

> ...not to be conceited or to fix their hope on the uncertainty of riches, but on God, who richly supplies us with all things to enjoy. Instruct them to do good, to be rich in good works, to be generous and ready to share, storing up for themselves the treasure of a good foundation for the future, so that they may take hold of that which is life indeed.

Much can be accomplished by even one person who has committed their resources to the Master's work. One of my acquaintances has a successful business and contributes over $1,000,000 per year to foreign missions. He possesses the ability to make money and longs to use it for the Lord's work.

One of the ministry tools I hope to develop from this book is a Christian Givers Network. I plan to develop a website which will encourage people to give to Christian ministries. This site will offer business and investment advice, business coaching from a Christian worldview, and a mentoring program for Christian business people. My goal is to provide a place for Christian ministries to tell about their work and meet givers who want to support God's work, as well as provide practical support for givers. Please accept my personal invitation to visit www.trueriches.net for details. If you are interested in being a part of the Christian Givers Network, feel free to contact me through the site.

In conclusion I hope you take these ideas and implement them as the Lord leads you. May the peace of Christ dwell in you as you dedicate yourself to serving Him.

EPILOGUE

Personal Invitation

If you have any doubt about your eternal destiny, please take a few minutes to read the following pages. I would like to tell you about God's plan for you to spend eternity with Him in heaven.

Jesus stated, "The thief comes only to steal and kill and destroy; I came that they may have life, and have it abundantly" (John 10:10).

Why don't most people have this peace and abundant life that God planned for us to have?

God is holy and just. No sin (evil or wrong-doing) can enter into His presence. He is the righteous Judge who is responsible to condemn sin. Each person on the earth has sinned. "For all have sinned and fall short of the glory of God" (Romans 3:23).

The punishment for that sin is death. "For the wages of sin is death, but the free gift of God is eternal life in Christ Jesus our Lord" (Romans 6:23).

Our sins stand between us and God. "But your iniquities have made a separation between you and your God, And your sins have hidden His face from you so that He does not hear" (Isaiah 59:2).

Men have tried since the beginning of time to reach God, but the Bible says that "all of us have become like one who is unclean, and all our righteous deeds are like a filthy garment;

and all of us wither like a leaf and our iniquities, like the wind, take us away" (Isaiah 64:6).

Nothing we can do is good enough to satisfy the perfection and holiness required for a relationship with God. But God was not content to allow us to live in bondage to our sins, then to die and face hell. As a Judge, He must execute justice. As a Lover, He chose to pay the debt for His loved ones. "For God so loved the world, that He gave His only begotten Son, that whoever believes in Him shall not perish, but have eternal life" (John 3:16).

Our redemption was purchased at a high price—the death of the Son of God. Jesus was holy and without sin, so He was able to become the sacrifice for the sins of the world. He paid the penalty for our sins when He died on the cross and rose from the grave. Jesus is the only Mediator through whom we can reach God. He is the only bridge between God and us. "For there is one God, and one mediator also between God and men, the man Christ Jesus" (I Timothy 2:5).

"Therefore, having been justified by faith, we have peace with God through our Lord Jesus Christ" (Romans 5:1).

"For Christ also died for sins once for all, the just for the unjust, so that He might bring us to God, having been put to death in the flesh, but made alive in the spirit" (I Peter 3:18).

"But God demonstrates His own love toward us, in that while we were yet sinners, Christ died for us" (Romans 5:8).

"Behold, I stand at the door and knock; if anyone hears My voice and opens the door, I will come in to him and will dine with him, and he with Me" (Revelation 3:20).

"But as many as received Him, to them He gave the right to become children of God, even to those who believe in His name" (John 1:12).

"That if you confess with your mouth Jesus as Lord, and

believe in your heart that God raised Him from the dead, you will be saved; for with the heart a person believes, resulting in righteousness, and with the mouth he confesses, resulting in salvation" (Romans 10:9-10).

When we make Jesus the Savior and Lord of our lives, we acknowledge the truth of 2 Corinthians 5:14-15: "For the love of Christ controls us, having concluded this, that one died for all, therefore all died; and He died for all, so that they who live might no longer live for themselves, but for Him who died and rose again on their behalf."

In summary, here is the path to God:

1. Admit your need to God for salvation (Tell Him: "I am a sinner").

2. Turn away from your sinful lifestyle. The Bible calls this repentance.

3. Believe that Jesus Christ died for you on the Cross and rose from the grave. Trust His payment for your sins to make you right with God.

4. Through prayer, invite Jesus Christ to come in and control your life through the Holy Spirit. (Receive Him as Lord and Savior.)

Are you ready to pray now and surrender your life to Jesus? If so, stop right now and pray. If you received Jesus Christ as Savior, the Bible says: "For whoever will call on the name of the Lord will be saved" (Romans 10:13).

"For by grace you have been saved through faith; and that not of yourselves, it is the gift of God; not as a result of works, so that no one may boast" (Ephesians 2:8-9).

When you make Christ your Lord, you are born into God's family through the supernatural work of the Holy Spirit who indwells every believer. This is called regeneration, or the new birth.

RAY TRAYLOR, CPA

If you committed your life to Christ, you just took the first step in your new life. Jesus wants to fellowship with you in your daily life. To deepen your relationship with Him you should:

1. Read your Bible everyday to know Christ better.

2. Talk to God in prayer every day.

3. Tell others about Christ.

4. Worship, fellowship, and serve with other Christians in a church where Christ is preached and the Bible is taught.

5. As Christ's representative in a needy world, demonstrate your new life by your love and concern for others.

If you have just made this decision, please e-mail me at ray@trueriches.net to let me know. I want to pray for you and offer the help you will need to grow in your fellowship with Christ.

THE ARROWS' NEW MUSIC RELEASE:
Justice Met Grace

The Arrows is a Christian brother/sisters singing group from north Louisiana. They sing the old hymns, praise and worship music, and a few contemporary Christian and country songs. They love to sing the hymns a cappella. They accompany themselves on the piano or guitar on their other songs.

The Arrows are Rachelle, Charissa, Jonathan and Jessica Traylor. They have been singing together as a group since 2000. Each of the group members was home educated from kindergarten through high school by their parents, Ray and Brenda Traylor. Each one of **The Arrows** is a committed Christian. They are dedicated to serving the Lord by worshipping and ministering in song.

Listen to the Music and Order a CD at
www.thearrows.org
Booking Manager: Rachelle Traylor
880 Bethel Church Road, Lillie, LA 71256
Phone: 870.863.9237 or 318.986.5279
Email: thearrows@thearrows.org

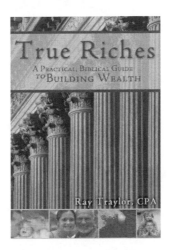

- Order additional copies of *True Riches*
- Schedule a financial seminar for your group or business
- Receive information about and sign up for Ray's business and financial coaching services
- Find out about Christian ministries that you can help support
- Submit information about your Christian ministry for consideration in the Giver's Network

www.trueriches.net
Toll-free (US): (888) 354-4912
Local: (870) 863-9237

Made in the USA
San Bernardino, CA
10 March 2013